Everyday ACTION Everyday CHANGE

This book is dedicated to our children and nephews — William, Logan and Hugo. You were our inspiration and give us hope for the future.

First published in Great Britain in 2023 by Wren & Rook

Text copyright © Naomi Evans and Natalie Evans 2023
Cover image copyright © Jasmin Sehra
Illustrations copyright © Kelly Malka 2023

All rights reserved.

The right of Naomi Evans and Natalie Evans and Jasmin Sehra and Kelly Malka to be identified as the authors and illustrators respectively of this Work has been asserted by them in accordance with the Copyright, Designs & Patents Act 1988.

ISBN: 978 1 5263 6509 5
1 3 5 7 9 10 8 6 4 2

MIX
Paper from responsible sources
FSC® C104740
www.fsc.org

Wren & Rook
An imprint of
Hachette Children's Group
Part of Hodder & Stoughton
Carmelite House
50 Victoria Embankment
London EC4Y 0DZ

An Hachette UK Company
www.hachette.co.uk
www.hachettechildrens.co.uk

Printed and bound in Great Britain by Clays Ltd, Elcograf S.p.A.

The website addresses (URLs) included in this book were valid at the time of going to press. However, it is possible that contents or addresses may have changed since the publication of this book. No responsibility for any such changes can be accepted by either the author or the publisher.

Contents

INTRODUCTION   9
When I Knew I Wanted to Be a Changemaker

THIS BOOK AND YOU   22

CHAPTER ONE   29
We Are All Different, and What We Mean by Prejudice and Discrimination

CHAPTER TWO   53
Everyday Actions of an Anti-Racist Changemaker

CHAPTER THREE   111
Everyday Actions Against Sexism, and Why Everyone Should Be a Feminist

CHAPTER FOUR — 129
Everyday Actions Against Homophobia, and Celebrating All Kinds of Love

CHAPTER FIVE — 157
Everyday Actions Against Ableism, and Creating a World for All

CHAPTER SIX — 177
Protecting Yourself from Burnout, and Looking Out for Yourself

BE A CHANGEMAKER — 191

GLOSSARY — 197

RESOURCES — 205

HELLO, EVERYONE

Firstly, we want to say a HUGE thank you for starting this book. Whether you have picked it up yourself or a friend or family member has given it to you, we are so happy you have begun your journey as a changemaker! We have written this book because we believe that everyone can make a difference in this world for good. There will be many different points in our lives – some when we will need to rest, some when we will need to talk to people about how we are feeling and others when we will need to take action. We wish we'd had a book like this when we were younger and that we could have chatted to our teachers, parents, caregivers and friends more openly about the world. So, we hope that this book will help *you* with some of those big questions and leave *you* wanting to ask more. And we hope it will help you to think about what you can do to look after yourself better, as well as helping other people. Don't let anyone make you think you can't be a changemaker.

LOVE,
NAOMI AND NATALIE

INTRODUCTION

When I Knew I Wanted to Be a Changemaker

NATALIE

When I was younger, I always knew I wanted to help change the world. **Sounds big, doesn't it?** But that really is what I wanted. And though I was determined to do something that would make a huge difference in my life and to those around me, I never knew what that looked like. I thought the only way I could make a difference was to be famous, because it felt like those were the only types of people others listened to and looked up to. So that's what I aspired to be – I wanted to be an actor or a singer, and I must have made this very obvious at the time because the year I left school, I was voted in our class yearbook as the **most likely to be famous**.

However, the older I became, the more I realised that being famous wasn't really something that inspired me any more: I didn't like the thought of everyone looking at me or the thought of not having a private life. But I still had that desire to **make a difference in the world**. The question was, **how could someone like me do something like that?**

You see, the reason I wanted to make a difference was because I felt different. I know that sounds strange, but hear me out . . . At school I had discovered a couple of things about myself that made me feel as if I wasn't like everyone else around me. The first thing was that **my skin colour was different from others'**. I didn't notice this until I went to primary school and realised I was the only person there who looked like me.

I AM MIXED RACE

My dad is Black and my mum is white. I have brown skin, big curly afro hair and brown eyes. What is really cool about being mixed race is that I have two heritages: **JAMAICAN** and **BRITISH**.

Jamaica is a beautiful country in the Caribbean — it's really, really hot! It has blue seas and white sand, and it never snows there. I have been to Jamaica a few times to visit my dad, who lives there, but I was born and always lived in the UK with my mum. I grew up in a town by the seaside with my sisters, Naomi and Rachel.

In the summer, we would play on the beach for hours and I loved making sandcastles and swimming in the sea with my friends. But I always felt as if I stood out — not a lot of people had the same colour skin as mine, so people would often stare at my sisters and me, sometimes also saying mean things to us, or about us to my mum, because we looked different. I found that really hard because I didn't understand why people couldn't accept me for me. At school, I struggled to remember what the teacher was telling me —

it sometimes felt as if things were **going in one ear and straight out the other** without my brain retaining the information. On top of that, I found it difficult to spell when I wrote, and I struggled with grammar and where I should put commas and full stops. I felt embarrassed when handing in my homework – I thought the teachers would read it and think I wasn't smart enough.

A MOMENT THAT HAS STUCK WITH ME MY WHOLE LIFE

Do you ever think about moments in your life that make you cringe? You might be lying in bed and suddenly this memory comes to your mind of something you did or said and you feel so embarrassed that you just want the ground to swallow you up! Well, this is mine, and I have never forgotten it . . .

'Right, everyone, we're going to do a test today!'

said my maths teacher. Everyone moaned and got out their pens. A test! I said to myself. **But I haven't revised!** I didn't know we had a test today. Remember when I said things at school went in one ear and straight out of the other? Well, I turned to my friend and said,

'Sophie, did you know we had a test today?'

'Yes, of course,' she replied. 'Haven't you revised?'

I replied, 'Yeah, obviously.'

I lied. And although I felt so nervous, I got through the test (phew!). Then a couple of weeks later when our maths teacher said, 'Right, everyone, I have the results from your test,' my heart began to beat really fast. 'There was just one person who failed the exam and won't be given a mark,' said the teacher.

PLEASE DON'T BE ME, PLEASE DON'T BE ME,

I thought to myself. 'And that person,' continued the teacher,

'is . . . NATALIE.'

Everyone in the class turned to look at me and laughed. At that moment, I felt so ashamed of myself. I laughed it off. I pretended I didn't care. But I did. I did care and it was devastating. From that moment on, I was really hard on myself. I decided I was the only person in the world who must be like this. And over time this made me feel alone and sad, and I began to *really* dislike school.

BUT THINGS GOT BETTER!

When I got a little older and went to college, things started to turn around. When I handed in my first piece of work, my teacher asked to see me. I remember thinking, *She's going to laugh at me. She's going to tell me off because of my spelling or my grammar* . . . But she didn't. She asked me if I had ever been tested for dyslexia. **'Dyslexia?'** I asked. **'What is that?'** My teacher explained to me that dyslexia is a learning difficulty that can affect reading, spelling and grammar. I couldn't believe it! Maybe I wasn't the only person on the planet to struggle with writing after all? This also explained why I struggled on my maths test at school.

Once I was diagnosed with dyslexia, everything was so much clearer. It was like someone had finally turned on the light switch. I could finally see what was around me, and it started to make sense! Now I know **I AM SMART ENOUGH**, and even though I still struggle with spelling and grammar, I know to give myself extra time when I am writing and to use the tools that are out there to help people who are dyslexic like me — such as computer software that helps me check my spelling and grammar, or lined writing paper, which makes it easier for me to read. I also know **to not be so hard on myself**.

WHY AM I TELLING YOU THIS?

I am telling you this because I grew up not seeing people who looked like me and not knowing that people had dyslexia like me. Not knowing I had dyslexia made me think that my dreams were impossible and that the only way I could be something or make a difference to the people around me was to be like everyone else. But now I know that's not true. Being me, and the only one of me, is **GREAT**! If you were born into a world in which you don't fit, it's because you were born to help create a new one.

THE THING THAT CHANGED OUR LIVES

Remember when we said we wanted to do something to help change the world? Well, that kind of happened, but not in any way we ever could have imagined. We're going to share this story with you now, but we just wanted to remind you that this is a very unique story, and it doesn't mean that to be a changemaker something like this has to happen. Being a changemaker is ultimately about the **little acts of kindness** we do and the way we think about the world and others.

NATALIE

One day I was on the train coming back from London when I saw a racist incident happen. We're going to talk a lot more about what **RACISM** is and how it shows up later, but for now, in case you don't know what racism is, here is a really short explanation.

Racism is when someone is treated differently because of the colour of their skin and their culture.

While on the train, I witnessed two white men say a racist comment to the train conductor (this is the person who checks your tickets on the train). The train conductor was a Black man and I chose to record what was going on because racism is a crime in the UK and I wanted to have some evidence to give to the police. But I also decided to say something to the two men, because I didn't agree with what had been said. I told the men that what they had said was **NOT OK** because it was **RACIST**. It was a very scary moment,

and no one else on the train spoke out apart from me. I was shaking, my hands were sweating and my heart was beating really fast. Even though I felt as if what I said didn't really make any sense, when I was finished, the two white men apologised. After the incident, I phoned my sister Naomi. I was upset and we both asked the question:

WHY DID NO ONE ELSE SAY ANYTHING?

A few months later, I decided to post the video online to share with my close friends and family to help them understand that racism happens in the UK every day and that it's important to speak out when you hear it.

The video went viral and was seen by over a million people. And that was when Naomi and I decided to set up our platform @everydayracism_ on Instagram. We now have over 200,000 followers, which is about the same as the number of people in two sold-out football stadiums!

EVERYDAY RACISM

EVERYDAY RACISM is a platform that helps educate people on racism. We write and design lots of posts about what racism is and how it can affect Black people and people of colour (the term **people of colour** refers to anyone who isn't racialised as white). We also write letters that people can use as a template to contact their local MPs. We decided to call the platform Everyday Racism because racism is something my sister and I have experienced throughout our whole lives. We want to help people who do not experience racism understand how harmful it can be to encounter.

WE WERE SAD THAT NO ONE ELSE SAID ANYTHING, BUT THEN WE REALISED WE COULD BE THAT SOMEONE!

We are now called **activists**. An activist is when someone fights, campaigns or raises awareness for change, and in our case, we are **anti-racist** activists. We fight for the rights of Black people and people of colour. What Natalie did was scary and brave, but it started our journey in making a real change in the world around us.

Of course, being a changemaker will look different for everyone. You don't have to publicly share videos of yourself or have a popular Instagram account to be a changemaker. And remember, you have to be over thirteen to create a social media account – but you know what? That doesn't matter, because everyone can create change, with or without social media. Whatever way you decide to make change, we are just so happy you are here to learn more. Because we believe everyone can help change the world, even you. **Yes, you!**

TOGETHER WE CAN REALLY MAKE A DIFFERENCE.

THIS BOOK AND YOU

Our hope for this book is that you will learn more about the issues many people face on a daily basis and master how to make the world a better place. You might be thinking, **'Well, what can I do?'** but there is SO much you can do – TRUST US.

At times, when reading this book, it might feel like a lot to take in. You might feel sad, or you may reflect and learn things about yourself that you didn't know, but this is all OK. **Your feelings are valid.** Along the way, we are going to explain what different words and terms mean when we are talking about injustices ('injustice' is when someone is treated unfairly), but sometimes you may forget what these terms are and that's fine – we have created a glossary at the back of the book.

Throughout this book, we'll give you lots of tips on how to spot and call out different forms of injustice. **But always remember that your safety comes first.** If you don't feel safe, it's better not to say or do anything. Instead, you could try to make a difference afterwards, for example, by reporting what happened to a trusted adult. Or you could check in with the person who was treated unfairly to see if they are OK. Just because you didn't say anything in that moment doesn't mean you can't still be a changemaker.

We will also be inviting some of our friends along to join us! They will pop up in different chapters to share their life experiences and what it's been like to feel different from others too.

WE CAN MAKE A CHANGE ONE STEP AT A TIME!

Throughout the book, we will give you some **EVERYDAY ACTION** tips that you can put into practice, and some **EVERYDAY MINDSETS** so that you too can be a **changemaker**.

EVERYDAY MINDSET

To start, we would like you to take part in our first everyday mindset. You could write down the answers to these or just think about them in your head.

WHAT WORDS MAKE YOU, YOU?

Think of or write down the first five words that pop into your head.

HERE IS NATALIE'S LIST:

Sister

Silly

Sociable

Auntie

Food

HERE IS NAOMI'S LIST:

Teacher

Mum

Fashion

Coffee

Giggly

WHAT IS YOUR SUPERPOWER?

We don't mean flying like some sort of superhero! We are referring to what is unique about you. It could be something that makes you different. Or it could be something you really like about yourself.

HOW COULD YOU USE YOUR SUPERPOWER TO HELP CHANGE THE WORLD?

This may seem like a really big question, but remember, no one else has to see this answer, so you can write whatever you want, even if it may seem absurd! It can be bold, it can be small — whatever you feel comfortable with.

OK, ARE YOU READY TO BECOME A CHANGEMAKER?

yes? Let's Go

CHAPTER ONE

We are all different, and what we mean by prejudice and discrimination

you eight BILLION PEOPLE

Did you know that we are all unique? But what do we mean when we say we're unique? You may not believe it, but there **ARE OVER EIGHT BILLION PEOPLE ON THE PLANET**. Yes, that's a lot of people making their way around the Earth, living their lives. And one of those people is YOU! What's more is that no one is the same as you! We're all one of a kind, but what is it that makes you, you? What makes us different from each other?

IDENTITY

Your identity is who you are as a person, and it's made up of many characteristics such as:

- **HOW WE LOOK**
- **THE WAY WE THINK**
- **OUR PERSONALITY**
- **WHERE WE COME FROM**
- **WHAT WE BELIEVE**
- **WHAT WE LIKE TO DO**
- **WHO WE LOVE**

A great way to think about identity is by picturing a puzzle. Now imagine each puzzle piece represents a part of your identity, and when you put them all together, they make you! Everyone will have different puzzle pieces and, let's face it, the world would be pretty boring if we were all the same!

THERE IS ONLY ONE OF YOU IN THIS WORLD, SO WHY NOT BE THE BEST VERSION OF YOU?

Sometimes identity can be fluid. This means it can **change** and **grow** over time, for example, the football team you support, your hobbies, the people you love or your beliefs.

Let's go back to our puzzle. In *this* puzzle, as you go through life, you may swap some pieces out and replace them with something else, and that's absolutely fine. It is a puzzle that does not have to keep the same pieces to be complete. There are some parts of your identity that you *can't* change, and these will stay with you forever, such as the colour of your skin or where your family is from.

Your values are also a really important part of your identity. Values are ideas you have or the areas in life that are meaningful to you. A value is a belief in something that shows what is important to you. Values also help you to see what you think is right and wrong. What's super cool is that your values can change as you learn and grow.

Here are some examples of values:

CREATIVITY

RESPECT

Remember when we said we are all unique? Well, this includes our values. Everyone has values that are unique or important to them, and this is really cool because it means we don't have to just see the world through our own views, but **we can learn from other people's perspectives too.**

VALUES HELP DIRECT US AND GIVE US MEANING AND PURPOSE IN LIFE

NAOMI

Here is a memory I have where I learnt about someone's else's values. At lunch one day at secondary school, pork with potatoes and vegetables was on the menu. There was a boy called Arman standing in front of me, who chose to have the vegetarian option. I asked him why he didn't want to eat the meat option. He told me that he was a Muslim and so he could not eat pork. I had never met someone who was Muslim before, so I asked him if he would share more with me about his faith.

33

He told me that Muslim people follow a religion called Islam, and that they believe in a god called Allah. He told me all about how Muslims pray five times a day (called Salah or Namaaz), and that the reason Muslims do not eat pork is because it is forbidden in the religion, according to the Qur'an (the holy book of Islam). Some of Arman's values were different to mine, but I loved learning more about him, and how his religion was a huge part of his identity and made up a lot of his values. It meant I got to know him better.

EVERYDAY MINDSET

Take a moment to think about your identity and values, and what's important to you.

Here are some questions to help you:

 Where do you live?

 What do you like to do?

 What makes you unhappy or sad?

 How do you think we should treat other people?

 What makes you feel excited?

WHERE DO I BELONG?

As you get older, some aspects of your identity will form a core part of who you are and it's quite common for these to become a label. Labels can be great because they help us to find community with others and with like-minded people – you might have experienced that already. **Do you have friends or groups of friends with whom you have things in common that bring you together?** It could be that you all support the same football team, that you all like the same music/band or that you have a shared hobby. Whatever it is, it's nice to know that people around you share the same interests. Even though labels can be super helpful, they can also make us feel pressured to use them. We may feel at times that we need to fit in where we don't feel comfortable.

NATALIE

When a friend of mine was at school, because she was very tall everyone assumed she would have excellent netball skills – they labelled her and made assumptions about her based on the way she looked.

What really matters is that we are comfortable with who we are and the labels we choose. It's not for anyone else to label you; only you know who you are and what makes you, **YOU!** Don't let anyone tell you otherwise.

Take a look at these words and see which labels you recognise and which you don't...

CLASS **RACE** **CULTURE** **NATIONALITY** **RELIGION** **GENDER** **AGE** **DISABILITY**

WE SHOULDN'T PUT OTHER PEOPLE IN BOXES

There are some people in this world who won't like or agree with your label or who dislike things about your identity and will be mean to you because of it. This is also known as **PREJUDICE** and **DISCRIMINATION**.

Prejudice is when someone has already pre-judged another person before getting to know them. This can be because of the way someone looks, acts, speaks or behaves. It's common to pre-judge a person when we first meet them – do you ever hear a little voice in your ear that says, 'Oh, they are pretty,' or, 'Wow, I like their top – maybe they have lots of money?' Well, this is how prejudice works. But what is important is that we must be careful not to treat people unfairly or differently based on our prejudices.

DISCRIMINATION is when we act upon our **PREJUDICES**. It can be when someone, or a group of people, is treated unfairly because of their identity. Discrimination happens every day – sometimes in small ways that build up over time, but other times in much more obvious ways. Often discrimination happens to marginalised groups of people. **MARGINALISED** people are those who are often prevented from accessing basic opportunities just because of their identity.

Remember I said at the beginning of the book that I was going to give you some everyday action tips? Well, here is one now...

EVERYDAY ACTION

Is there something you can do in your life to help others learn more about discrimination and prejudice? Remember that you don't need to be the expert. Maybe while you're learning more about how prejudice and discrimination show up, you could bring your friends or family along with you?

Here is an idea: how about implementing or developing a system in your school, for example, a lunchtime book club where you read books about social injustice and action?

CAN YOU THINK OF ANYTHING ELSE?

Here are some stories of people I know from marginalised groups who have been discriminated against:

MEET MYRA

Myra is a friend of ours who is ambitious, talented and fantastic at her job. One day she has the opportunity to apply to be a manager at her work, which is really exciting! She is super qualified for the job and the interview goes really well. They talk about salary and she is offered less than what she thought she would get. She is a little upset as she has all the qualifications and experience they asked for. She says she will think about it, and when she leaves the room she goes into a lift where she sees another work friend, Ben, who has also interviewed for the job. He hasn't been at the company for as long as Myra and is less qualified. They are talking about the interview and Myra discovers that he was offered £5,000 more than she was offered.

In this case, Myra was discriminated against because she is a woman. Women have historically been marginalised because of their gender and have been seen as less important than men.

MEET SIMON

Simon is a friend of ours who is disabled, and because of this he has to use a wheelchair. One day Simon and his Auntie Helen go to a festival to see his favourite band. Before Simon bought tickets for the event, Helen checked the website to see if the festival would be accessible for people who use wheelchairs. **It said it was. It also said it would have a viewing platform so that people who use wheelchairs could see the stage.** Unfortunately, when they arrive at the festival, there is no viewing platform for Simon to use and he has to watch the stage from the back of the crowd, which makes it really hard for him to see as everyone is standing in front of him. The event organisers had decided not to put the viewing platform in because it would cost too much money.

Simon was discriminated against because he is disabled and uses a wheelchair. He is also marginalised because of his disability and treated differently to those who are able-bodied.

MEET REBECCA

Rebecca is Muslim so she wears a hijab to cover her hair. **Rebecca loves playing football and she is an excellent striker – not only does she think this, but all the people she plays with say she is.** Rebecca decides she is going to try out for her local football team. On the day, they have to do a series of trials, including shoot-outs, keepie-uppies and taking part in a football match. Afterwards, the coaches talk to each person individually and ask them questions. Rebecca is asked if she can play without her hijab, to which she answers, **No. It's against my religion.** The coaches say to her that she can't be on their team unless she removes her hijab, and this means she is unable to make the team.

Rebecca was discriminated against and is marginalised because of her religion.

It seems really unfair that this happens, right? A good thing is that in some countries, including the UK, **acts of discrimination are illegal, to make sure that people are treated fairly.** However, discrimination is not always taken seriously and those who make laws or enforce sentences can sometimes be people who do not experience discrimination on a day-to-day basis. This means they often won't understand what it feels like, or recognise the seriousness of it when it does happen. This is why it's really important to **learn about other people's experiences** even if it doesn't affect you personally, because then when discrimination shows up, you can recognise it and know how to stand up for people – **which is exactly how we can be changemakers!**

EVEN IF IT DOESN'T AFFECT US PERSONALLY, WE SHOULD STILL CARE

Sadly, in some other parts of the world, there are no discrimination laws in place and people are discriminated against every day. There can be big limitations on what they can do about it, which is why it's vital that, where we can, we speak up on behalf of those who can't do so themselves. There are many different names given to how discrimination shows up. Some of them you may have heard of before. Take a look at these words and see which ones you recognise and which you don't. If you want to learn more about what any of these terms mean, turn to the glossary on page 197.

RACISM

ABLEISM

TRANSPHOBIA

ANTISEMITISM

HOMOPHOBIA

SEXISM

CLASSISM

SINOPHOBIA

ISLAMOPHOBIA

EVERYDAY ACTION

Is there someone you know who is facing discrimination? Maybe it's a friend at school who is being picked on? Or a family member? Or is it someone you heard about on TV?

Why not do something nice for them to let them know that you support them and care about them? **It could be writing them a letter to cheer them up.**

Whatever it is, spend some time thinking about what you can do to make someone **smile** today.

While many of us face discrimination because of our identity, we can also experience **privilege** because of our identity. Privilege is when a person has certain advantages because of aspects of their identity.

IMAGINE A DINOSAUR AND A DRAGONFLY

The dinosaur and the dragonfly are the best of friends – **they do everything together**. One day the dinosaur and dragonfly decide to go to a new pizza place in town. However, when they get there, the door is **REALLY small**. Now, the dragonfly is small enough to fly straight through the door, but the dinosaur is way too big and can't fit. As much as he tries, he can only get one foot

43

through the door. The dragonfly is really hungry and becomes impatient.

'**Come on**,' says the dragonfly to the dinosaur. '**I am hungry.**'

'**I can't fit**,' says the dinosaur. '**I am trying, but I can't get through. Can we just go somewhere else?**'

The dragonfly gets really angry and says, '**Why do I have to go somewhere else just because you don't fit?**'

The dinosaur responds, '**I am sorry. Some places are just not set up for me, and I can't access the same places as you can because I am too big.**'

Hearing this, the dragonfly feels bad and starts to think about all the places they can go to because they are smaller and because they can fly. The dragonfly realises it's a lot more places than the dinosaur.

'**I am sorry**,' says the dragonfly. '**I have never had to think about places I can or cannot go because of my size, and I have realised that's because of my privilege. Let's go somewhere else.**'

'**That's OK**,' says the dinosaur, and off they go to another pizza place that is more inclusive and where the dinosaur can fit inside and enjoy a lovely pizza.

And so you can see, some people are given things in life to help them just based on their identity. This can include someone's gender, body size, skin colour, ability, education, culture, religion and many more.

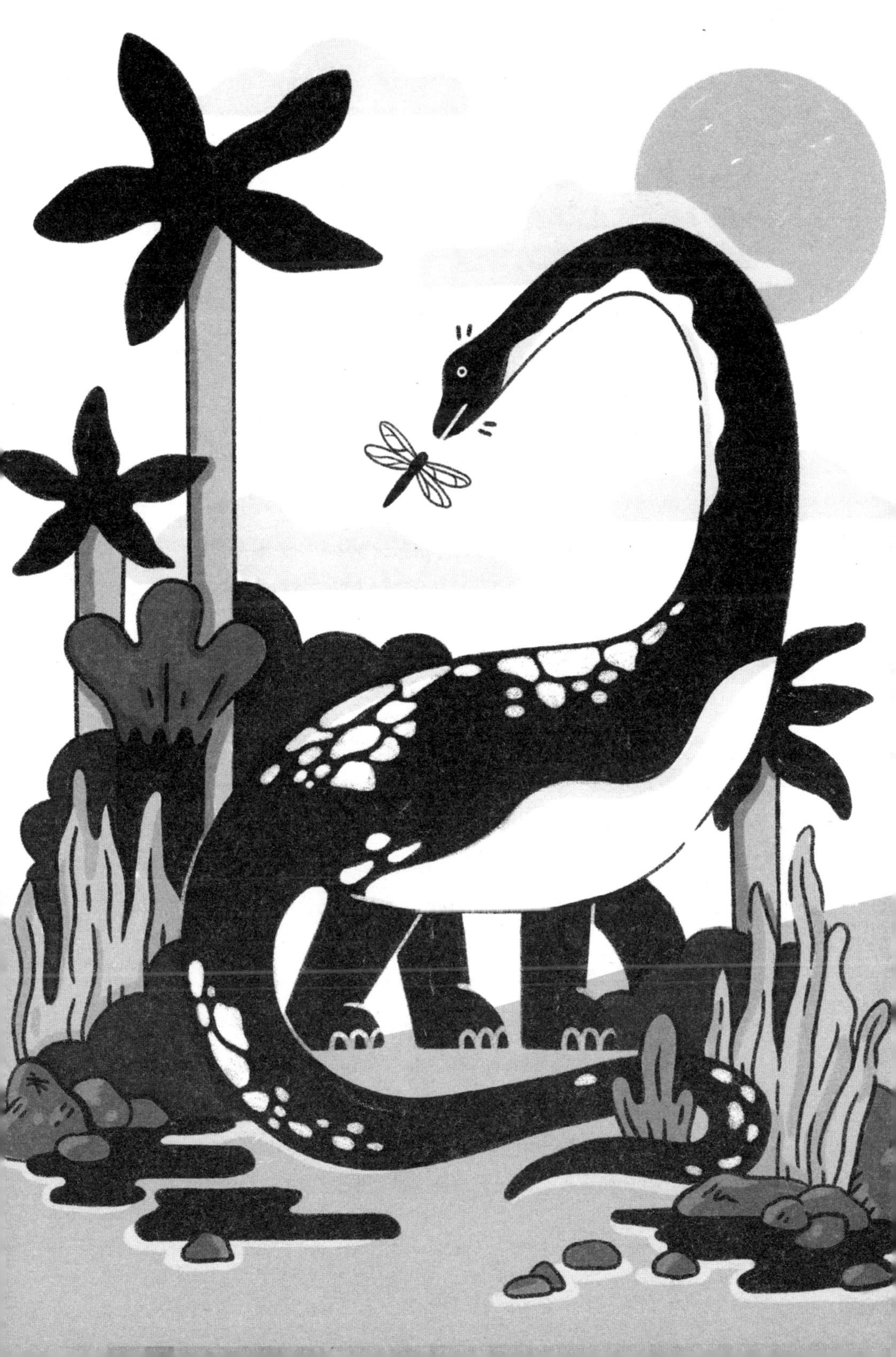

LIFE ISN'T THE SAME FOR EVERYONE, SO WE MUST LEARN FROM ONE ANOTHER TO HELP ONE ANOTHER

The next stop on our grand tour of identity is **intersectionality**. This big word is broken down like this:

inter-section-ality

It was a term used by **Professor Kimberlé Crenshaw** to help us understand that **we all have our own unique ways of experiencing discrimination and privilege**. Kimberlé is a Black woman and she noticed that there wasn't a useful way to talk about the fact that the experiences of Black women are different to the experiences of white women.

> You see, women can face **sexism**. Sexism is the way men and women are treated differently. (Women have historically been treated badly and not had the same rights as men.) As a woman, Kimberlé has faced sexism (she has been treated differently because of her sex), but as she is a Black woman, she also faces racism.

You could think about it like this: if you are Asian and identify as a girl and you don't have a **disability**, you may experience racism and sexism, but you won't face **ableism** (discrimination against you because you have a disability). Or if you are a boy who is white and gay with a disability, you may face homophobia and ableism but not racism.

The important thing about intersectionality is to remember that **life isn't the same for everyone**, even those who share similar identities as you, and by understanding how intersectionality works, **we have a better understanding of how to help others**.

THESE ARE SOME FACTORS THAT MAKE UP INTERSECTIONALITY

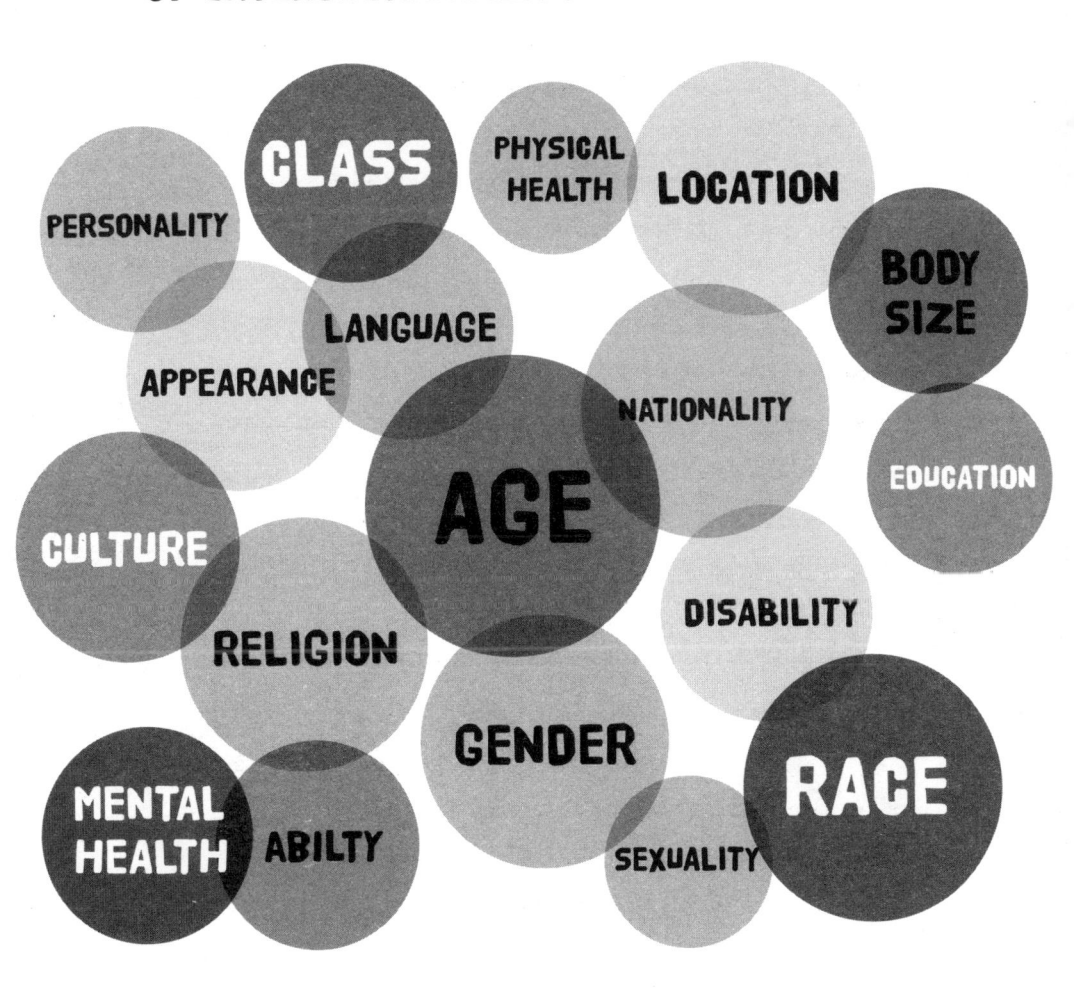

- PERSONALITY
- CLASS
- PHYSICAL HEALTH
- LOCATION
- BODY SIZE
- LANGUAGE
- APPEARANCE
- NATIONALITY
- EDUCATION
- AGE
- CULTURE
- DISABILITY
- RELIGION
- GENDER
- RACE
- MENTAL HEALTH
- ABILTY
- SEXUALITY

EVERYDAY MINDSET

What is something that you have seen or experienced in the world that is unfair?

✦ How did it make you feel?

✦ Did you feel confident enough to say anything?

✦ If it happened again, what would you do differently?

That was a lot we just went through, wasn't it? And there were some really big words. Don't worry if you don't quite understand what they mean yet – it will take time.

Feel free to take a pause or a break here if you need it. We know it's a lot to take in!

PAUSE ⏸

One of the most important words on the planet is ... empathy. Have you ever heard of it? Empathy means the ability to understand other people's feelings and experiences, even if you're not facing the same thing. **Here are some examples of empathy in action:**

You got the part you wanted in the school play, but you find out that your friend didn't get the part they wanted and they are really upset. Even though you got the outcome you wanted, you still feel really sad for your friend. **This is empathy.**

You're at a friend's birthday party and you're watching them open their presents. Your friend told you beforehand that all they wanted for their birthday was a specific game for their Nintendo Switch. When opening their presents, they finally get it, and you are so happy for them! Even though you didn't buy it and even though it's a game you wouldn't have asked for, you're still chuffed for your friend. **This is empathy.**

EMPATHY IS CARING ABOUT AND RESPECTING SOMEONE ELSE'S FEELINGS

Another part of empathy is being able to understand someone else's way of thinking even if you don't agree with them. It's a way of seeing something from a different point of view. You may have heard the phrase '**putting yourself in someone else's shoes**', and this is exactly what that means. Here is an example:

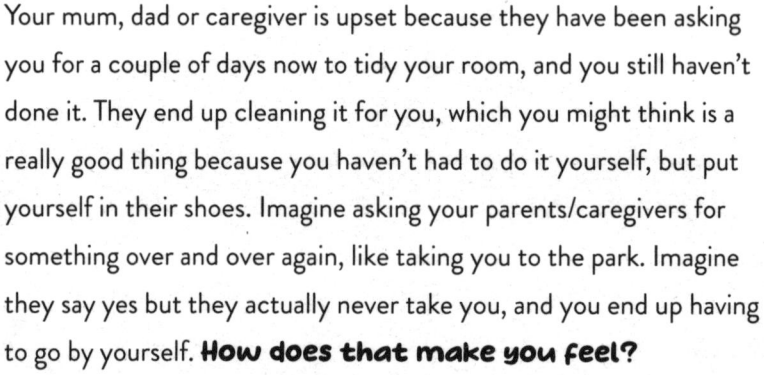

Your mum, dad or caregiver is upset because they have been asking you for a couple of days now to tidy your room, and you still haven't done it. They end up cleaning it for you, which you might think is a really good thing because you haven't had to do it yourself, but put yourself in their shoes. Imagine asking your parents/caregivers for something over and over again, like taking you to the park. Imagine they say yes but they actually never take you, and you end up having to go by yourself. **How does that make you feel?**

HOW CAN YOU PRACTISE EMPATHY?

Empathy is about not only what someone else is feeling, but also caring enough to do something about it. Practising empathy helps you to be a better friend and a more caring person.

EVERYDAY ACTION

Here are some everyday ways we can practise empathy:

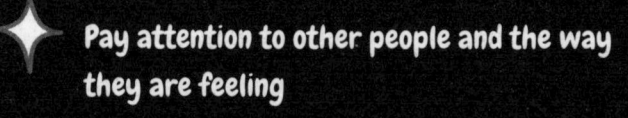

- **Pay attention to other people and the way they are feeling**

- **Think before you speak or act**

- **Remember that everyone is unique**

- **Stand up for others**

REMEMBER!

Empathy doesn't mean you will always 100% understand what someone is going through, but it's about taking the time to think about what life is like for different people, because we don't live in a world that is fair for everyone.

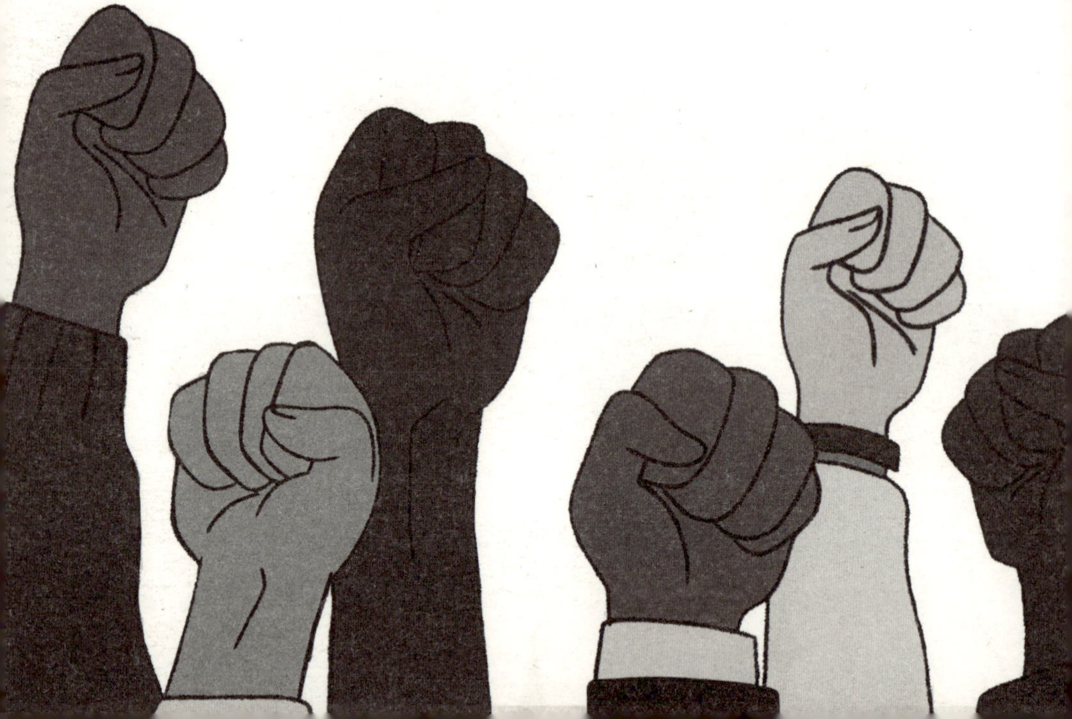

CHAPTER TWO

Everyday actions of an anti-racist changemaker

CHANGEMAKERS

Did you know that there is a difference between not being racist and being actively anti-racist? In this chapter, we're going to be talking about what that difference is and how to be an anti-racist activist, changemaker and **ally** in your everyday life. Now, the word anti-racist might seem unusual or it might be a term you haven't heard before, but trust us, everyone can be anti-racist and it takes far less work than you might think. In fact, we can all do it on a daily basis. Before we go into what an anti-racist is, let's talk about what it means to be racist and the many ways this shows up.

WE MUST BE ACTIVELY ANTI-RACIST IN ORDER TO MAKE CHANGE

NATALIE

The first time I experienced racism was when someone said something really mean to me at school about the colour of my skin. They said something to me that they would not have said to anyone who had white skin, and it was hurtful. I soon learnt that racism was really common and I knew other people who had experienced it too. One of my cousins, who is Black, told me that no one would play with her at school because of the colour of her skin. Another cousin told me he had been attacked because of his skin colour.

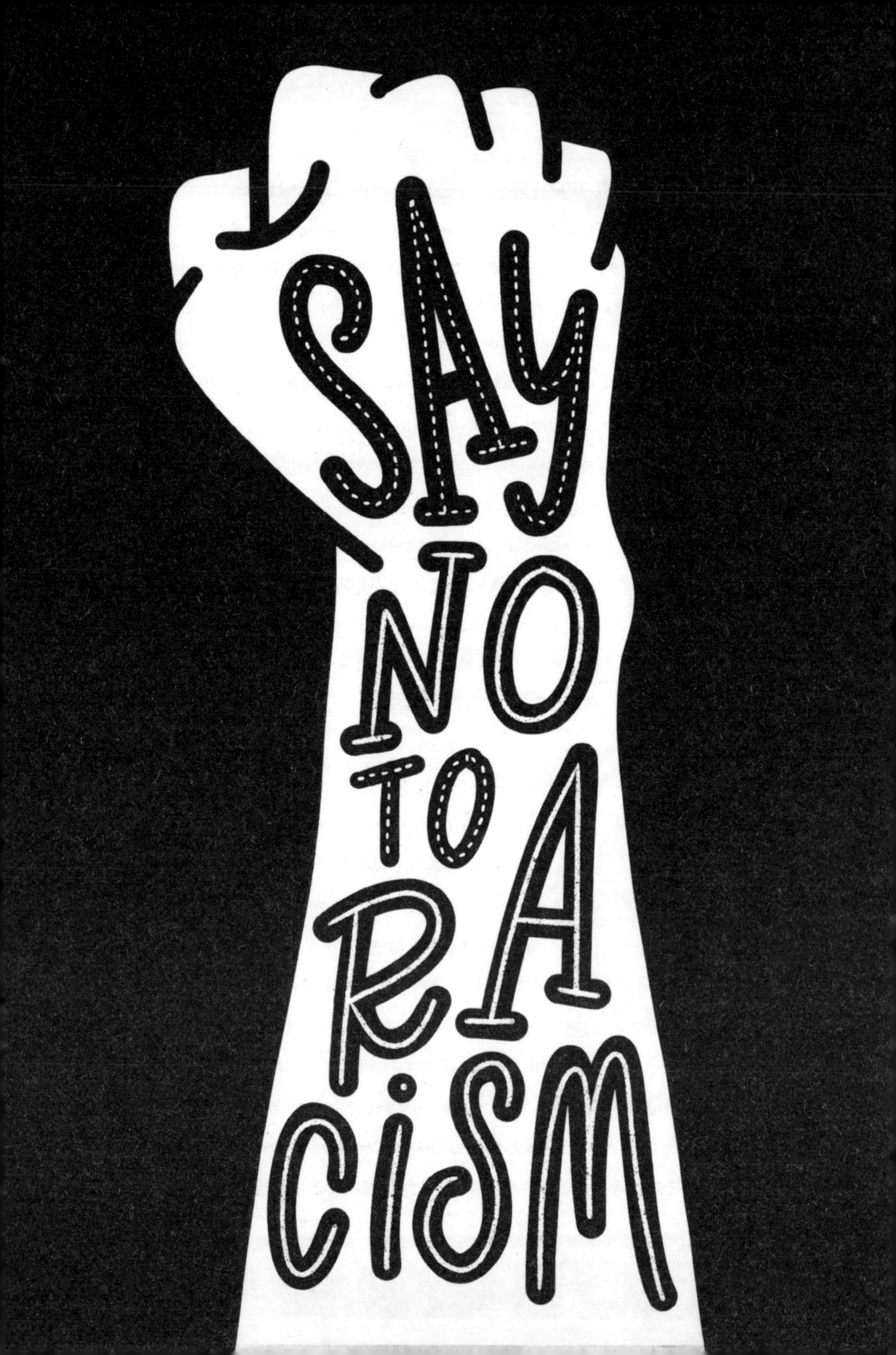
SAY
NO
TO
RA
CISM

The simplest way to understand racism is this: **it's when someone is discriminated against because of the colour of their skin, their culture or the language they speak.**

Though it most commonly occurs through words, racism isn't always something you can see or hear. Sometimes you feel uncomfortable about a situation because you know you're being treated differently to other people. Racism can affect our daily lives in many different ways. Sometimes people are called unkind things, refused opportunities or made to feel they can't be themselves. Breaking it down into three categories can be helpful to figure out what kind of racism you are dealing with, and then to work out what steps to take to be anti-racist when you tackle it.

1 The first one is **INDIVIDUAL RACISM**. This is when racism is carried out from one person to another. There are many ways this can happen, including saying something mean to someone else, making a joke, asking rude or intrusive questions or having negative thoughts towards another person purely because they come from a different racial group. At its most extreme and dangerous, individual racism can result in physical violence or verbal abuse. I know this may sound really scary – unfortunately, the world can be a scary place at times. But do you know what is really cool? **We have the power to help change the way the world works if we all do our little part.**

2 Next up is **SYSTEMIC RACISM**. This is where organisations treat people with different colour skin unfairly. This isn't as much about one person being mean to someone else, instead it's about a group or organisation – for example, the police, schools or workplaces, and how they treat groups of people. Systemic racism can happen when racist ideas are built into policies, laws, attitudes and behaviour.

Here are some examples of this:

Black people and people of colour are more likely to be suspended from school.

Black people and people of colour won't read as many stories or watch as many films with positive examples of people who look like them as white people.

It might be harder for Black people and people of colour to get a job or progress in certain industries.

Black people and people of colour are more likely to be stopped by the police.

On top of this, the difficult thing about systemic racism (which can also be referred to as **institutional racism**) is that it's very hard to see. It can sometimes be invisible, and unless you look really carefully for it, you may not even know it's there or that something is wrong, especially if you benefit from it. **But the good news is, once you do see it, it's difficult to ignore, and that means we can do something about it!**

Something that helped us to understand systemic racism more was when we watched a video by Pop'n'Olly called 'Privilege Explained for Kids', which showed **how privilege works by using shapes**. This also works when trying to understand systemic racism.

Imagine you have a square, a circle and a triangle:

Now, imagine you are a square. But everywhere you go, everything is triangle-shaped. When you walk through the school door or play in the park on the swings, they are all triangle-shaped. This is great for those who are triangles and it is super easy for them to move through life because of it. But as a square, it's really hard for you to fit through the triangle shapes, and you are also treated unfairly and differently because you don't look like a triangle and because the world is set up for triangles. But triangles don't even think or see that anything is wrong. This is what systemic racism is like for Black people and people of colour.

3 Finally, we have **INTERNALISED RACISM**. This is when Black people and people of colour don't like themselves or something about themselves because of their race, ethnicity or culture. This is because of the negative messages they might see or hear about themselves, which results in them not liking who they are.

Again, imagine you have a square, a circle and a triangle.

Imagine this time you are a circle and the world is set up for squares. Every time you watch TV, open a book, go to school or hang out with your friends, everyone is a square and people laugh at you for being a circle. After a while you might start to not like being a circle and want to be a square instead. You will start to do everything you can to not be a circle and you may even start to dislike yourself. This is how internalised racism works.

EVERYDAY ACTION

In order to help fight racism, we must be active in how we respond when we hear or see racism. There are many ways we can do this, but here are some actions we can take:

ACTION

Acknowledge your privilege. Think about the ways your life is different because you don't experience racism.

Correct yourself if you say or do something offensive that hurts someone else.

Turn away from people who make racist jokes or comments

Identify where you can show up for your friends when they experience racism – what are some things you could say or do?

Observe and listen to your friends' lived experiences of racism, and remember to not push for answers – ask your friend first to make sure they don't mind talking to you about racism.

Never stop learning about the experiences of Black people and people of colour and how racism shows up – why not read some books about Black history or other books written by people of colour that talk about their personal experiences?

If you're someone who does experience racism, remember:

> IT IS NOT YOUR RESPONSIBILITY TO EDUCATE OTHERS ABOUT RACISM – UNLESS YOU WANT TO.

> WHO YOU ARE IS VALID AND YOU ARE ENOUGH.

> TALK TO SOMEONE YOU TRUST IF YOU DO EXPERIENCE RACISM.

> PRACTISE SELF-CARE.

REPRESENTATION IS IMPORTANT BECAUSE IT CAN HELP US FEEL SEEN AND INCLUDED

NAOMI

When I was younger, I loved reading books and watching programmes and films with princesses in them, and one of my favourites was *The Little Mermaid*. But I never saw a brown-skinned mermaid or princess in the books I read or on TV, so I ended up wanting to be white because I thought that would make me more like a princess. It's taken me a little while to understand that this was internalised racism, but now, I love being me, and what has helped me to love the colour of my skin is seeing more and more people who look like me on TV and in books. I was so happy when I learned that in the 2023 version of *The Little Mermaid*, Ariel is Black.

CAN YOU BE RACIST WITHOUT MEANING TO BE?

The short answer is yes. **We all have prejudices.** Sometimes they come from things other people, such as family and friends, have told us. Other times it's from things we hear on the news or read in the media. Prejudice also comes from a place of ignorance and not knowing much about a particular group of people. That's why the important parts of being an anti-racist are being open minded and being willing to learn from others. **We might change our minds and form our own opinions about things as we grow, and that's OK.**

EVERYDAY MINDSET

Think of a time when you have had a negative thought about someone. It could be because of the way they looked, what they were wearing or an assumption about that person that wasn't true.

✦ Think about where those thoughts came from.

✦ Why did you think that?

✦ Was the thought true?

UNCONSCIOUS BIAS

Have you ever thought that some of the problems in the world could all go away if people just thought the way you did? Everyone in this world has so many different points of view, and some of these we don't all agree on. **Bias is when we have formed a judgement or an opinion on someone or something before we have even got to know them.**

Unconscious bias is even more tricky because this is when people don't even know they have a bias towards someone and don't notice they are causing someone harm; this can also be known as ignorance. Unconscious bias can occur because of many reasons, such as where we have grown up or what other people have told us. Someone might grow up in a house where they hear racist things being said and so they form the same views without realising.

Here is an example:

Imagine you're at the airport. You're super excited to be getting on a plane soon, but before you do, you decide to get some food. As you walk to the restaurant, you bump into someone who is cleaning the floor — you say sorry and carry on.

You arrive at the restaurant and the person working there takes you to your table. You have a lovely meal and tip the person who served you, then you leave to catch your flight.

As you get on the plane, the pilot stands at the door and says, 'Hello.' You say, 'Hello,' and take your seat. Then a member of the cabin crew comes over to offer you a drink. You say, 'Thank you.' Finally, your flight takes off and you're looking forward to your holiday!

Now we want you to think about everyone you just met in that story . . . the cleaner you bumped into, the server at the restaurant, the pilot, the member of the cabin crew. What did they look like?

What if we told you the cleaner was a white man, the server at the restaurant was a man in a wheelchair, the pilot was an Asian woman and the cabin crew member was a Black man? Spend a few seconds thinking about what the people looked like in your head when you read the story. Did you assume they looked a different way?

IT IS IMPORTANT TO BE AWARE OF OUR BIASES AND TO LOOK FOR WAYS WE COULD BE HURTING OTHERS BECAUSE OF IT

EVERYDAY MINDSET

Try writing down or thinking of a reason why it's important we keep checking our biases. Here are some examples:

✦ It's important I keep checking my biases because then I don't cause harm to others

✦ It can help me to learn and grow

✦ It will help me to stop making assumptions about others

✦ Can you think of any others?

MICROAGGRESSIONS

This may seem like a really big word, but don't worry, we are going to break this down for you. **Microaggressions** are when a person says something to or acts in a certain way towards another person or a group of people, which implies something negative about them. It is very common for microaggressions to be aimed at people who are in marginalised groups. Microaggressions usually happen because someone is trying to be polite or give a compliment but it actually ends up doing the opposite. It can also be a subtle way of being racist – sounds a little confusing, right? Well, this is the problem with microaggressions. It's sometimes hard to know when you are saying something hurtful or offensive, which is why microaggressions can be really upsetting. The very reason they are called 'microaggressions' is because 'micro' means small and this usually means they are delivered in a way that doesn't seem like a big deal.

Some examples of microaggressions can be . . .

> **BOYS CAN'T WEAR NAIL VARNISH.**

> **YOUR NAME IS HARD TO PRONOUNCE.**

> **YOU DON'T ACT LIKE A GIRL.**

You might be reading this and thinking, *But these aren't mean things to say, are they?* Or you might be reading this and thinking, *This happened to me, and I wasn't sure why I was upset.* **This is why microaggressions are so important to understand – they can seem harmless, but they are actually really hurtful.** Imagine you're camping in the woods and you get bitten

> YOU SPEAK ENGLISH SURPRISINGLY WELL.

> CAN I TOUCH YOUR HAIR?

by a little insect – it's obviously not a nice feeling to be bitten by a bug and it can feel a bit uncomfortable and itchy at times. It won't affect your camping trip, though, because you can still play with your friends or eat marshmallows by the fire. However, what if you get bitten by these bugs over and **over and over and OVER AGAIN** until your body is covered in insect bites? By then it would hurt and you would feel very uncomfortable – you might even have to go to hospital. Now imagine the insect bites are microaggressions; one little comment isn't nice, but hearing that same comment over and over again can make you feel really sad or even angry.

NATALIE

When I was at school, everyone would touch my hair. I have beautiful curly hair and because no one else had hair like mine, everyone else wanted to touch it — some people touched my hair without even asking. Even though they weren't being really nasty to me, having other classmates and teachers touching my hair every day made me feel isolated — I felt singled out because of my hair. I wanted to straighten it so no one would touch it again.

EVERYDAY MINDSET

Write down or think about a time when you made a mistake.

✦ How did it make you feel?

✦ What did you learn from that mistake?

HOW TO BE AWARE OF MICROAGRESSIONS

Some microaggressions are much easier to recognise as harmful than others, so how do we know if we are hurting other people? One way is to ask ourselves the following questions:

- **WHY AM ASKING THIS QUESTION OR SAYING THIS COMMENT?**

- **HAVE I MADE ANY ASSUMPTIONS ABOUT THIS PERSON?**

- **HOW WILL THIS MAKE THE OTHER PERSON FEEL IF I ASK OR SAY IT?**

Sometimes people might *tell* us that what we said or did is racist. That won't feel very nice. But it's in these moments that we should learn and listen to other people.

EVERYDAY ACTION

We ALL make mistakes, and that's OK as long as we learn from them and attempt not to make them again. If someone does call you out for saying something offensive, try some of these phrases:

✦ Thank you for letting me know, and it's something I didn't realise was offensive.

✦ I am sorry for making you feel that way, and it's something I am trying to understand better.

✦ Is there anything I can do to make sure I don't do or say that again?

WE DON'T KNOW WHAT WE DON'T KNOW. HOW DO I DEAL WITH A MICROAGGRESSION WHEN IT'S SAID TO ME?

Because microaggressions can take you by surprise, it's hard to know how to deal with them when you hear them. One thing I have found really helpful is **to think about how you would like to respond in that situation**. This will depend on some different factors, for example, will you be safe if you respond at that moment?

REMEMBER, YOUR SAFETY IS THE MOST IMPORTANT THING, so make sure you have people around you to support you; ask an adult to help you if needed and don't challenge people on your own – especially people you don't know. Do you need to do it in person or could you write something down? Always use a 'me' or 'I' statement, for example:

> 'WHEN YOU SAID ____ IT MADE ME FEEL ____'

If you're at school or somewhere with an adult present, always tell a person you trust what happened, and if it's the adult who said it to you, make sure you tell someone else.

And remember, it's OK if you don't say something in the moment. If you want to, you can always come back to it later or when you have someone with you who can help you deal with it.

I CAN SEE WHERE RACISM SHOWS UP, BUT WHERE DOES IT COME FROM?

Racism all started because some people believed they were better than others based on the colour of their skin. This is also known as their **RACE**. Race refers to the physical characteristics that define you and make you a part of a group, for example, skin colour, hair colour and hair texture. The word race is thrown around a lot, but did you know that race doesn't actually exist?

Yes, that's right. It was something invented around the seventeenth and eighteenth centuries to divide people. Various people proposed different versions of race, including a man called Johann Friedrich Blumenbach, who decided to split people into five categories:

Caucasian, the white race

Mongolian, the yellow race

Malayan, the brown race

Ethiopian, the black race

American, the red race

> It's important to remember that these terms are not used any more, and we should never use these terms to describe anyone's race.

By putting people in different categories and using that to say the white group was the most powerful, it allowed people to say that the white group *should* have power over all the others. This meant that things like slavery and mistreating other people could be justified. In the past, scientists even suggested that Black people were less intelligent than or not equal to white people. This meant that they were treated differently or that people made assumptions about what they would be like.

Another way we talk about racism is by using the words **white supremacy**. White supremacy is a belief that people who fit the category of white are superior to others and should be given lots more power, particularly when they have lots of money as well. But we now know that race doesn't even exist, so no one should be seen as better than anyone else.

THE SIMPLE FACT IS THAT THERE IS ONLY ONE RACE:

the HUMAN race

WHY DO WE HAVE DIFFERENT SKIN TONES?

The science behind why we have different skin tones is fascinating. The human race all started with dark skin tones. When humans ventured out of Africa tens of thousands of years ago, they went to all different parts of the world. Our skin has small cells called melanocytes, which create melanin (black and brown skin pigments). A person's skin colour is determined by the amount of melanin they have. When the sun is bright, melanocytes produce a lot more melanin. All of us have melanin in our skin, but people who are born in or who have parents from sunnier countries will have more, which makes their skin darker.

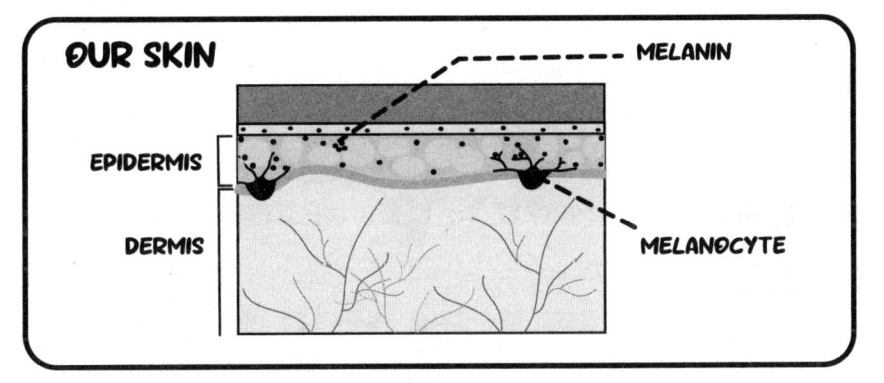

OUR SKIN

- MELANIN
- EPIDERMIS
- DERMIS
- MELANOCYTE

WHY DOES IT MATTER WHAT WE LOOK LIKE?

Well, the fact is it shouldn't matter. We all have the right to be ourselves. It shouldn't matter how we look, how we dress, how we speak or what size our body is, but sadly people often make judgements and treat us differently based on these things. Can you remember what this is called? That's right: **prejudice** and **discrimination**.

When a person is pre-judging a group of people or an individual based on assumptions, we can call this a **stereotype**.

A stereotype is when we have an idea or belief about groups of people. Stereotypes can be dangerous because they can suggest that people behave in certain ways or that they can or can't do certain things. Have you ever been told that the colour pink is just for girls? Or the colour blue is just for boys? That's because people often believe the stereotype that girls like the colour pink and boys like the colour blue, but of course we know that anyone can love whatever colour they want!

HERE ARE SOME EXAMPLES OF STEREOTYPES

- IF YOU DON'T OWN YOUR OWN HOUSE, YOU DON'T WORK HARD ENOUGH.
- ALL PEOPLE FROM AFRICA ARE POOR.
- PEOPLE WITH BIGGER BODIES ARE LAZY AND EAT JUNK FOOD.
- PEOPLE WHO DON'T SPEAK LIKE THE QUEEN ARE NOT VERY INTELLIGENT.
- GIRLS ARE NOT VERY GOOD AT FOOTBALL.

HOW DID RACISM SHOW UP IN THE PAST?

Major historical events have shown us how badly groups of people have been treated because of the invention of race. We are going to take you on a little journey through history now.

Some of what we will share with you might be hard to read, so why not read this section with an adult you trust so you can learn together and talk to them more about it?

It's important that we learn about the past so we don't make the same mistakes again in the present.

ENSLAVEMENT

As far back as the fifteenth century, Black people were kidnapped and taken from their homes in Africa. They were transported on ships with appalling conditions so they could be sold as slaves. This was because Black people were not seen as human beings but as property to be bought and sold. Countries such as Britain, Portugal, Spain and France organised the trafficking (illegal trading) of people to countries like the United States of America and Brazil, where they were forced to work, for example, on plantations to pick cotton or sugar in order to make money for their white owners. It is believed that over twelve million men, women and children of African heritage were forced into slavery. While slavery was abolished (officially ended) in the nineteenth century, the impact of how Black people were treated is still being seen today.

THE HOLOCAUST

The Holocaust is an example of genocide. Genocide is the mass murder of large numbers of people because of their race, religion or ethnicity. During the Second World War (1939-1945), the Nazi party, which was led by dictator Adolf Hitler, oversaw the Holocaust – one of the most terrible events in human history – which led to the mass murder of European Jews and other groups of people.

There are Jewish communities all over the world. Many Jews are religious, and there are several different religious movements within Judaism, the religion that Jews follow. Many other Jews consider themselves ethnically or culturally Jewish but don't believe in God. The Nazis created extermination camps in which Jewish men, women and children were made to live and work in horrific conditions. Many were killed on arrival, while others died from starvation and illness. By the end of the war, the Nazis had murdered approximately six million European Jews—a third of the world's Jewish population. Hitler also persecuted and killed at least five million prisoners of war, Roma and Sinti people, Jehovah's witnesses, gay people, disabled people and Black people.

As the war came to an end in 1945, the Nazis tried to destroy the camps to hide evidence of what they had done. Each year, in countries all over the world, there is a Holocaust Remembrance Day to ensure what happened is never forgotten and to prevent genocide in the future.

Today, Jewish people still experience antisemitism. Antisemitism is the name for racism against Jews.

SEGREGATION

The word **segregation** means to deliberately separate people from each other. After enslavement (the act of making someone a slave) in the United States became illegal in 1865, there were still other ways that Black people were persecuted. Several laws were passed in the southern states of America which meant that Black people were kept separate from white people and had fewer rights. This happened in many places, such as schools, buses, trains and waiting rooms, and some cities even banned Black people from moving into areas where white people lived. Then, in 1954, the Civil Rights Movement began – when Black people came together to fight for segregation to stop.

MARTIN LUTHER KING JR

"I HAVE A DREAM."

You may have heard of the very famous activist and minister Martin Luther King Jr, who delivered a speech called 'I Have a Dream'. Alongside Martin Luther King Jr were hundreds and thousands of people fighting for the rights of Black people and equality. This movement lasted many years, and sadly people were killed during this time, including Martin Luther King Jr. Because of this movement, some of the segregation laws began to be overturned, but unfortunately the impact of segregation is still seen today.

APARTHEID

In South Africa and South West Africa (which is now called Namibia), there was another form of legal segregation called apartheid. New laws were introduced in South Africa after the National Party won the election in 1948, and they divided areas into 'Black' and 'White'. Legal segregation meant that people had to do certain things otherwise they would be sent to jail. People were told who they could marry, who they could be friends with and even the places they could or couldn't go to. This was in order to keep Black and Brown people separate from white people.

There were many uprisings and protests to try to end apartheid. One of the most prominent leaders of these was Nelson Mandela, who was arrested in 1962 for trying to overthrow the government. After many years of campaigning, apartheid ended in the early 1990s, and Nelson Mandela was freed from prison. In 1994, all people were allowed to vote and Mandela became the president of South Africa.

COLONIALISM

Colonialism is when one country takes over the lands or borders of another. It can happen for different reasons, for example, when a bigger country wants more power and so uses force to take over smaller countries, or when it wants something from the land of that country that will make money, like oil or metals.

Have you ever wondered why so many countries speak English even though England is a small country in comparison to so many others? It's because of something called the British Empire. In the sixteenth century, Britain began to take control of other countries and use their resources for its own benefit. Over the years Britain took control over parts of Africa, Asia, North America and Australia. It was there that Britain built what we call 'colonies'. The biggest injustice was, however, that there were already people living in these countries and they were treated very badly, either by being forced to move off their land or by being enslaved and forced to work to create power and wealth for the British Empire.

WE STILL FEEL THIS TODAY

The impact of these events is still being felt today. There are many groups of people and individuals who have been held back in their education, their ability to make money and their health because of these events – this is also known as systemic racism **(remember that from earlier?)**. Because power and money are still held by a lot of the same people, they haven't been shared properly between everyone, so the fight for equality continues.

RACISM NOW?

We asked some people to share their own experiences of racism in their day-to-day life. Here's what they said:

- I wore my hair in my natural afro to school. I was told by the teacher that I had to sit at the back of the class because my hair was getting in the way of students being able to see to the front of the classroom.

- Another student at my school told me they think people who weren't born in England should go back to their own country.

- My mum cooked traditional Sri Lankan food for my lunch and people at my school made fun of me and said it smelt funny.

- I've never had a teacher who wasn't white, and sometimes that makes me sad because I'd like to see someone who looks like me in my school.

- My mum's boss made a joke about her looking like a terrorist. She wears a hijab and so do I.

- Once I wore a sari to my friend's birthday party and everyone made fun of me.

THESE AREN'T SMALL THINGS

If you've experienced things like this in your life, they can make you feel excluded, angry and upset. It can also be hard to know who to talk to, and that's why it's important to understand how racism works, so we don't add to the problem. It can also be hard when someone talks to you about racism and you don't understand it or you didn't mean to upset them. **So what should you do if you've said something in the wrong way or hurt somebody?**

EVERYDAY ACTION

Here are some things you can do if you have hurt somebody:

Listen to the person you upset.

Exercise empathy.

Apologise and accept accountability.

Remember: this moment isn't about you; it's about the other person.

Note that this incident happened and write down, or think about, how you would stop it from happening again. In other words...

LEARN FROM IT!

BLACK LIVES MATTER

BLACK LIVES MATTER

You have probably heard the term **Black Lives Matter (BLM)** or you might have even been on a protest. Maybe you have heard people around you talking about the organisation or perhaps saying negative things. That is often because it's not widely known why the BLM movement started back in 2013. In 2012, a Black teenager in America called Trayvon Martin was shot and killed by George Zimmerman in a racially motivated attack. Zimmerman lived in the area and thought that Martin looked 'suspicious'. After a lot of campaigning, Zimmerman was arrested for the murder, but on 13 July 2013, a jury found him not guilty and he walked free. Many people felt this was another example of how Black people's lives in

America are not valued in the same way as white people's, and three women, Alicia Garza, Patrisse Cullors and Ayo Tometi, who had children themselves, got together to start a protest. The organisation has grown significantly and works to help support Black people in their communities. People all over the world recognise #BLM.

ISLAMOPHOBIA

Islamophobia is one type of discrimination based on religion and in this case it's fear, hatred and violence towards people who adhere to the Muslim faith. Islam is the name of the religion, and a follower of the faith would be referred to as a Muslim. Did you know that around a quarter of the world's population is Muslim? While anyone from any race can be Muslim and follow Islam as a religion, the majority of the Muslim community come from Black and Brown communities, so the prejudice they experience is often also racial prejudice. Some people blame Muslims for terrorist attacks that have happened; however, these were carried out by extreme groups that claim to be Muslims and instead use it as an excuse for their abhorrent actions. It is unfair that a whole group of people is blamed for something a small number of individuals have done.

SINOPHOBIA

Sinophobia is discrimination against, fear of or hatred of the Asian country China, its people and its culture. Sinophobia can be traced back to the 1800s, when Britain said that the people of China were uncivilised. Britain and China went to war over trading terms (this led to the Opium Wars), and a lot of Chinese people were mistreated. Since then we have seen Sinophobia play out in other countries, such as Japan and Korea. Examples of Sinophobia include laughing or joking about people's facial features, people's accents or the food Chinese people eat. The most recent example was in the COVID-19 pandemic, where people blamed Chinese people for the virus and there was a huge increase in Asian hate and hate crimes.

CLASSISM

Classism is when people are treated differently based on their social status. There are different words used to describe what class we belong to, and the three most common ones are working class, middle class and upper class.

Working class people: This includes those who may not have a college or university education. The term is usually applied to people who went straight to work after they left school. Some of the jobs working class people will do are things like being factory workers, delivery drivers, restaurant workers and construction workers.

Middle class people: This group tends to have a higher level of education – for example, going to college and or getting a university degree – than working class people. They usually have more income available for spending, and they most likely own their own home or a type of property.

Upper class people: This term refers to those who are highest on the class ladder (however, this doesn't include aristocrats, i.e. the royal family). They will have the highest status in society and will have a lot of wealth. This means they may hold a lot of power in certain areas, such as politics.

Social class can contribute to the opportunities we may be given in life – for example, job opportunities. Some jobs might be offered to those who look and sound a certain way and appear to be upper class, meaning those who are in a lower class category sometimes might find it harder to apply for the same jobs.

There are lots of problems with having these categories and one of them is that some people make lots of judgements about others based on their class background, and this is how classism manifests. Always remember there is more to us than our class status, and no matter what your background is, you can still achieve great things.

IS IT RACIST TO TALK ABOUT OUR DIFFERENCES?

Some people take the 'colour blind' approach to racism. This is where they pretend that everyone is the same and that if we treat everyone the same there will be no inequality. Of course, it's important not to make judgements about people based on the way they look or speak, but it seems a bit silly to pretend that we don't notice things about people, right? We don't always need to make a comment on it, but there's nothing wrong with noticing that someone has white skin, brown skin or black skin.

NAOMI

Let's look at it like this. If I saw somebody with green hair walking down the road, I would probably notice, because I don't know many people with green hair. I don't need to run up to them and say, 'Oh wow, you have green hair!' but it would be strange to pretend I didn't see it. There's nothing wrong with talking about differences, as long as we aren't being negative or disrespectful about other people's appearances, cultures and traditions. I love learning about how other people live their lives!

When I was in my twenties, I left England and travelled to some different countries. **I met lots of new people and saw how other people lived.** In Thailand, I met fishermen who lived on the beach, and in Jamaica, I lived up in the mountains where I could pick mangoes and coconuts off the trees to eat. Lots of people enjoy sharing information about their own cultures, and if you're interested, you can investigate for yourself. **One of the most beautiful things about our world is how we all have differences, yet we have so much in common too.** I am a product of two cultures coming together, which I really love. **I love having family from different places too.**

EVERYDAY ACTION

Why not learn more about other people's differences, such as their culture? Here is an action you could do:

Ask your school to organise a culture day, where everyone brings in something about their family's culture and traditions. Maybe people could bring in food or wear traditional clothing.

WHY ARE RACISM AND HAIR LINKED?

There are certain types of hair that are seen as 'normal', and this means if your hair doesn't fit in with that, you might feel pressured to change it. When I was younger, I was the only person with hair like mine at my school. It was an afro texture and didn't lie flat. All my friends had silky straight hair, and lots of the people that I saw in magazines and on television were the same. It left me thinking that I had strange hair. It was also very difficult to find a hairdresser who knew how to cut and style my hair. Some of the adults at my school would just touch or stroke my hair, saying things like it looked like 'candyfloss'. It made me self-conscious and I spent a lot of time trying to get it to look like everyone else's.

BLACK HAIR IS DIVINE AND DESERVES RESPECT.

BLACK HAIR IS DIVINE AND DESERVES RESPECT

Did you hear of the story that came out in 2021 about swimming caps? For the Olympic Games, which took place in Tokyo, a company designed a swimming cap especially for some types of Black hair. Have you ever noticed that swimming caps are quite small and fit tightly to the head? But what about people who have thicker or bigger hair? Well, the international swimming federation (FINA, Fédération Internationale de Natation), who make decisions about swimming competitions, wouldn't accept the newly designed cap, suggesting it was unsuitable. This affected a lot of Black people who have afro hair.

It's sad that racism and hair are linked, but one of the ways we can counteract that is by **celebrating and learning about the wonderful and interesting history of Black hair**. We must also make sure that we respect afro hair by never touching someone's hair or making comments about people's hairstyles. **Black hair is so beautiful and amazing – it deserves everyone's respect**.

EVERYDAY MINDSET

Wow! There was a lot we just went through there, right? Before we move on, I would love you to reflect on what we have just learnt together. Write down or think about some of the key things that stood out to you. It could be:

- New information you learnt

- Something you read that made you feel happy or sad

- Something you want to learn more about in your own time.

WHAT IS AN ALLY?

An ally is someone who is there to join your side and support you, and who is willing to learn more about you so they can fight your corner.

If you are not a person of colour, you can be an ally to people of colour. There are lots of things in the world that are unfair, and a lot of these things happen to people in marginalised groups, so an ally helps make the world a fairer place for these communities.

Being an ally is all about action. It's about helping and supporting other people. It's about continually **showing up and using the privileges** you have. It's sometimes about **standing up for people who can't stand up for themselves**, but we must remember it's not about personal gain, so we have to listen to the people and communities we are trying to help and not talk over them.

Being an ally will look different for so many people, and there are many ways you can be an ally. Sometimes you need to speak out loudly for others to hear; other times you need to give up your privileges and step out of the way to let others speak. It will also depend on where you are in life, and how much you can do depending on your age. There are other elements too, such as how much money you have – some people can afford to donate to charities or support marginalised communities financially while others can't. You may be someone with a physical disability, which means it's hard for you to actively go out to things like protests. For lots of reasons, being an ally can be easier for some people than others. **However, whatever our circumstances, there is always something we can do to help others – which is great!**

"It is not enough to be non-racist, we must be anti-racist"

WHAT IS AN ANTI-RACIST ALLY?

An incredible activist from America called Angela Davis once said, **'In a racist society, it is not enough to be non-racist, we must be anti-racist.'** It's about **doing something to change the systems** and the way Black people and people of colour are treated; **it's about long-lasting changes.**

BE A CHANGEMAKER EVERY DAY!

The first step to becoming an ally is to **listen to and learn from** the people who you want to be an ally to.

Imagine you have been chosen as a dancer for a school production. The show is in a few weeks' time, but you don't show up to any rehearsals. It's the night of the performance, and you stand on stage and start dancing, but you're completely out of time with everyone else and you end up looking really silly, and it might feel like you have ruined the performance for everyone else.

Well, this is what it's like when we jump in head first and don't listen to other people's experiences. **We must try to take the time to understand what life is like for others**, especially when it's something we don't understand very well; otherwise it's possible we will talk over other people and take up spaces we shouldn't.

EVERYDAY ACTION

There are many ways we can learn about other people's life experiences... Try finding some TV programmes or films to watch, or read some books. Here are some suggestions to get you started:

WATCH:
- Diary of a Future President
- Mira, Royal Detective
- Motown Magic
- Over the Moon
- Coco

READ:
- The Girl Who Stole an Elephant by Nizrana Farook
- When Life Gives You Mangos by Kereen Getten
- The Stars Beneath Our Feet by David Barclay Moore
- The Proudest Blue by Ibtihaj Muhammad with S.K. Ali
- A Kids Book About Racism by Jelani Memory
- Antiracist Baby by Ibram X. Kendi
- We're Different, We're the Same by Sesame Street

What's even better is reading books written by authors who are Black or people of colour and then sharing them with your friends!

Once you start listening and learning from people who are different to you, it will be much easier to speak out when you hear negative things being said.

DO THE WORK

Can you think of a time when you were playing with your friends and one of them said something mean to another? Did you say anything at that moment? Did you feel too uncomfortable?

Speaking out loud can be really scary, right? Especially when you're saying something that no one else agrees with or going against what your friends may think. You might worry that you'll lose friends or that you might be the one who gets picked on next – but being an ally is about **standing up for what is right** and being a friend to those around you who are treated unfairly. However, it's important to remember that when speaking out, you must make sure your own safety comes first. We will go through this in the next everyday mindset.

SO HOW DO WE SPEAK OUT?

Speaking out doesn't have to mean having an argument with someone. It's just about sharing your thoughts on a situation and helping people to recognise when they are causing harm to others.

Here is an example: You invite two friends who don't know each other to your house to play some games on the Xbox. The game is so much fun, but there are only two controllers, so one of your friends is waiting their turn. But the friend you're playing with doesn't want to share their controller with your other friend. They say:

> **I DON'T WANT TO SHARE MY CONTROLLER WITH MUSLIMS.**

You know this is a really horrible thing to say and you see your friend looking sad, with tears in their eyes. In this moment, this is where you can be an ally – if I were there, I would say:

> **WHAT'S WRONG WITH BEING A MUSLIM? I AM FRIENDS WITH EVERYONE REGARDLESS OF THEIR RELIGION AND I WOULD LIKE ALL MY FRIENDS TO HAVE THE SAME MORALS, OTHERWISE I CAN'T BE FRIENDS WITH YOU ANY MORE.**

The friend who said the horrible comment says sorry and passes the controller over to your other friend.

There is a possibility that the friend who said the nasty comment remains defensive and doesn't want to apologise. In that moment, you could say, for example:

> **I DON'T PUT UP WITH PEOPLE BEING RACIST AROUND ME, AND IF IT'S SOMETHING YOU ARE GOING TO CONTINUE TO DO, THEN WE CAN'T HANG OUT ANY MORE.**

EVERYDAY MINDSET

Here are some things to remember when you speak out.

✦ Think about when the right time is to speak out. Is it safe? Where are you? Who is around you?

✦ Should it be in public or can it be done privately?

✦ It's OK if we don't speak up every time, but think about why you didn't and what you would do differently next time. Speaking out might not be as bad as you think.

PUTTING WORDS INTO ACTION

Have you ever felt so angry about something that has happened that you just don't know what to do with your anger? It's like a fire inside your belly that makes you want to scream. Well, this can be because of injustice and feeling helpless – but guess what? We can put these emotions into action in so many different ways.

Here are some examples . . .

PROTEST

A protest is when people come together and demonstrate whether they are for or against an idea or action. A protest is a very important way to make a difference, and historically protests have had a **significant impact** on how we live our life today. Some protests get a lot of attention from the media, and there are others that you may not have heard of but have still had a big impact on the way we live. Protests can take many different forms, from people refusing to do something to marching on the streets. Many protests are to get people in positions of power to **listen to a different point of view or to influence changes**.

GEORGE FLOYD AND BLM

You might have heard about the murder of George Floyd in 2020. George Floyd was a Black man who was arrested and killed by police in America. News about his death spread all over the world because the incident was filmed and the footage was shared on social media – and this drew attention to the unfair treatment of Black people at the hands of the police. Many people who had experienced racism in their life **felt more confident to speak out**, and there were **WORLDWIDE** protests, which demanded that the lives of Black people should matter as much as everyone else's. You may have seen these protests take place or even been a part of them. They were

GEORGE FLOYD

a **VERY POWERFUL** moment in our history and show us that when people come together, change can happen. Many companies, organisations and individuals began to **make changes** and **educate themselves** more about racism and prejudice because of the amount of people speaking out.

THE STONEWALL RIOTS

The Stonewall Inn is a famous bar in America. On 28 June 1969, people from the **LGBTQ+ community** (we talk more about the LGBTQ+ community in chapter five) were hanging out when police raided the bar and started arresting people. Fed up with not having a safe place to be together, people protested against this unfair treatment. **They wanted to be treated equally and to feel safe**. And guess what? After this, LGBTQ+ rights started to be taken more seriously in America. Though there is still a long way to go, this is an example of how coming together and protesting **can create change**.

THE SALT MARCH

The Salt March took place in 1930 in India. It was to protest against Britain ruling India. Under this rule, Britain wouldn't allow Indians to collect or sell salt, which was an important part of their diet. Instead, the salt had to be bought from the British. Gandhi was one of the people to head this protest. **MILLIONS** of people joined ongoing protests and tens of thousands were arrested. Seventeen years later, India was granted its independence from Britain.

EVERYDAY ACTION

We all have skillsets that we can use to support others. What could your superpower be to help raise money for a good cause?

- Could you wash cars for people?

- Could you bake cakes and do a bake sale?

- Could you do something where people sponsor you?

- What are some other fundraiser ideas that you can think of?

NATALIE

When I was younger, I did a sponsored sleepathon – I asked people to sponsor me to stay awake all night. I asked friends to join in too, and we raised lots of money, which we donated to a homeless charity.

NOTE: it's important to remember that this was something I did to help raise money, and staying awake all night is not something anyone should be doing without a parent's or caregiver's consent, and it should not be done on a regular basis.

EVERYDAY ACTION

What about joining some community projects in your area?

There may be lots of projects in your local community that you can get involved in or help organise, such asking your school to celebrate Black History Month and bring in people from the community to share their experiences.

YOU HAVE THE CHANCE TO CHANGE THE WORLD AND MAKE IT A BETTER PLACE.

MEET RUBY BRIDGES

At the age of six, Ruby Bridges became a history-maker who inspired people all over the world. Ruby grew up in Louisiana during the 1950s —when Black children in some states were not allowed to go to the same school as white children. This was because of racism and segregation.

THEN **NOW**
RUBY BRIDGES

Aged just six years old, Ruby passed an exam that meant she was allowed to go to an all-white school. On 14 November 1960 she was escorted by police marshals through the front doors of the school, walking past protestors who shouted racist abuse at her (protestors who didn't agree with integration). Ruby faced a lot of racism during her time at school and it must have been incredibly hard for her and her family.

Ruby went on to graduate high school, marry, have four children and work as a travel agent for fifteen years. In 1999, she published a book about her experiences, called *Through My Eyes*. She also founded the Ruby Bridges Foundation, which promotes equal opportunities and creates change through education.

RUBY BRIDGES

'WE MAY NOT ALL BE EQUALLY GUILTY. BUT WE ARE ALL EQUALLY RESPONSIBLE FOR BUILDING A DECENT AND JUST SOCIETY'

- RUBY BRIDGES

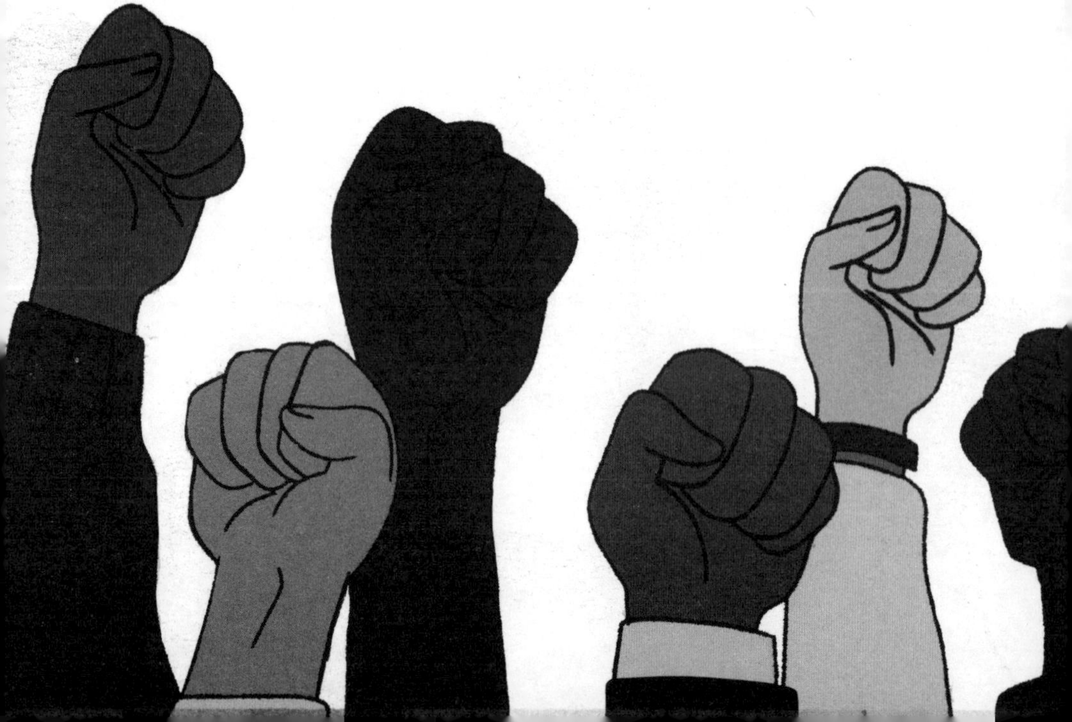

CHAPTER THREE

Everyday actions against sexism, and why everyone should be a feminist

EQUALITY

NAOMI

Remember when we spoke about labels in chapter two? Well, growing up, I was given labels that were about me being a girl. I was told that I was going to be so pretty when I was older, that I was such a polite girl, that I was very quiet. These would have been fine if they were all true! You see, I was sometimes polite – but quiet? No! I was loud and liked to be the centre of attention, so these labels that people put on me weren't really who I was – they felt like they were what people expected me to be. The older I got, the more I realised that this was a common theme among lots of girls and women I knew. I also noticed that women didn't have the same rights as men and that there was a wage gap, known as the gender pay gap. Did you know that, as of 2022, women in the UK earn around 15% less than men do? Doesn't seem fair, does it?

WE MUST CONTINUE TO FIGHT FOR EQUALITY

'THERE IS NO LIMIT TO WHAT WE AS WOMEN CAN ACCOMPLISH' - MICHELLE OBAMA

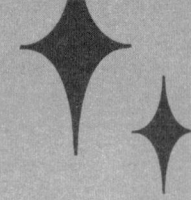

Equality is about making things equal, so that everyone is on the same level. It's about giving everyone the same tools to do the same job.

This sounds brilliant and it's a world we would like to be. However, this isn't always helpful for everyone and it can be seen as a quick fix, so that's why we need **EQUITY**. Here is an example of equity:

Imagine you and your friends have gone to watch a football match. You're all standing behind a fence to watch the game, but you are all different heights. The tallest friend can see the game without any issues. However, you and another friend are much shorter and are struggling to watch the match as the fence is in the way.

Now imagine this: you have all been given a box to stand on to help you see the match. You are being treated **EQUALLY**. One of your friends is a little bit taller than you, so now they can see the match by standing on the box. The friend who was tall enough in the first place

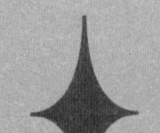

EQUALITY

can see the match, but you still can't see because you are shorter than both of them.

Finally, imagine this: you are given two boxes to stand on. Your slightly taller friend is given one box and your tallest friend isn't given a box because they are tall enough to see already. This is called **EQUITY**.

EQUITY

Equity is about giving everyone equal access to watch the game by meeting everyone's needs, and not just assuming that everyone needs the same thing. It's about seeing us all as individuals. The truth is, giving everyone the same thing only works if we all start from the same starting point, but as we have learnt already, not everyone does.

These illustrations are inspired by 'Illustrating Equality vs Equity': Interaction Institute for Social Change | Artist: Angus Maguire.

EVERYDAY MINDSET

Think of a time when you weren't treated equally to someone else.

✦ How did that make you feel?

✦ What could have been put in place to make you feel equal in that situation?

LET'S TALK ABOUT SEXISM

Sexism is when a person is treated unfairly because of their **sex** or **gender** (you can learn more about the differences between these terms on page 134). Unfortunately, women have historically been treated badly in comparison to men – they haven't had the same rights as men, which has led to many moments of protest and campaigning to ensure equality. This is mainly due to gender stereotypes, as well as beliefs about what girls and women should and shouldn't do.

Here are some examples of

GENDER STEREOTYPES

WOMEN SHOULD STAY AT HOME AND LOOK AFTER THE CHILDREN.

BOYS LIKE BLUE AND GIRLS LIKE PINK.

GIRLS ARE NOT AS GOOD AT SPORTS.

WOMEN ARE BETTER AT COOKING.

IN VIDEO GAMES OR FILMS, GIRLS ARE WEAK WHILE BOYS ARE THE HEROES, ALWAYS SAVING THE GIRLS.

BOYS WILL BE BOYS.

YOU MAY ALSO HAVE HEARD THESE SEXIST PHRASES . . .

MAN UP.

STOP GETTING YOUR KNICKERS IN A TWIST.

STOP BEING SUCH A GIRL.

You'll be surprised to find out that some people may still have these views or say these phrases today! What's more is that these beliefs have held some women back and even impacted their rights.

> **Did you know that it wasn't until 1928 in the UK that all women could vote in elections? Did you know that before 1970, it was legal in the UK to pay women less for doing the same job as a man?**

EVERYDAY MINDSET

Take a moment to think about a time when you might have experienced sexism.

✦ How did it make you feel?

Or think about a time where you might have said something sexist to someone else.

✦ How do you think that person would have felt?

EVERYDAY ACTION

Here we want to give you some everyday actions to help you when you next hear a sexist comment. These tips can help even if the comment is not directed at you – they will help you to stand up and speak out, and to be an ally. So, if you feel comfortable speaking out, then why not learn these phrases to help you:

- I don't think that's a fair/cool/kind thing to say.

- What you said is sexist and I don't agree with that.

- What you said made me feel _____ . And next time I would prefer it if you didn't say that.

WE CAN ALL WORK TOGETHER

The good news is that sexism is something we can all work together to fight, no matter what our gender is. One way we can do this is by being a **feminist**.

NATALIE

When I started to hear the word feminist, I always felt that lots of people associated negative feelings with the word. I would hear phrases such as 'feminists are just women who are being difficult' or 'all feminists hate men'. However, when I got older, I started to learn more about what feminism means and realised these phrases were simply not true.

WHAT IS BEING A FEMINIST?

Being a feminist just means you want all genders to have equal rights and opportunities – i.e. for *women to have the same pay as men; to be taken seriously for certain jobs that people think only men should do; to have the right to make decisions about their own bodies; to make the choices women want to make rather than men making choices for them.* Who wouldn't want that, right?

EVERYDAY MINDSET

Take the quiz on the opposite page...

ARE YOU A FEMINIST?

DO YOU WANT ALL GENDERS TO HAVE EQUAL RIGHTS AND OPPORTUNITIES?

YES   **NO**

WHOOP! YOU'RE A FEMINIST!

OK, let's look into this a little more.

EQUAL RIGHTS

Feminism started with the intention of making sure women had human and equal rights – this dates all the way back to the eighteenth century. Here are some of the feminist movements that have happened in history:

1800s-1900s

This period saw the birth of the women's rights movement – mainly in the US, UK and Canada. This movement focused on **WOMEN'S SUFFRAGE**, which means to have the **right to vote** and also have **legal rights**, including the right to simply buy a house.

At this time, women protested by holding large banners outside places like the White House in America and the Houses of Parliament in the UK. Some women went on a hunger strike and didn't eat until people listened to their demands (but it's important to remember that hunger strikes are very dangerous and children should not do this). **The protestors won – they won the right to vote, own houses and get an education.**

1960s-1980s

This movement started in the US and then spread to Europe and Asia. It was about **gender equality**, including closing the **gender pay gap** and **fighting for rights over women's**

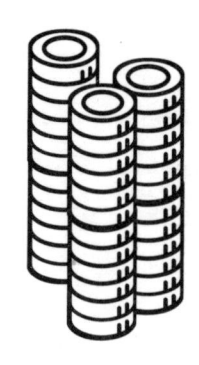

bodies – not letting men tell women what they could or couldn't do. This included things like the right to decide to have babies or not. In 1970, the **EQUAL PAY ACT** was introduced in the UK, which helped stop companies from discriminating against women.

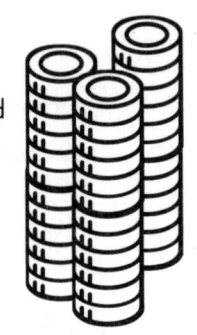

1990s-NOW

Believe it or not, women continue to fight for their rights, and now more than ever are focusing on inclusivity and making sure feminism is for all. Remember that big word we used in chapter two – **intersectionality**? Well, this word is very important when looking at feminism, because some women feel they are excluded from the movement. Black women, women of colour, transgender women, disabled women and other marginalised women have felt they were not included and that feminism really only focused on white women. Now the movement is trying to be much more intersectional and include everyone.

The cool thing about feminism is that it was a **MOVEMENT FOR CHANGE**, and it shows how we can all be changemakers. We can always do things by ourselves, but it is even **more powerful** to do things together as a group!

THE MORE PEOPLE ARE INVOLVED, THE STRONGER YOU CAN BE!

EVERYDAY MINDSET

Spend some time thinking about what feminism looks like for you.

✦ What does it mean to you?

✦ How would you describe a feminist?

✦ Who does it include?

EVERYDAY ACTION

What are some things you can do to be a feminist?

Challenge people when they say things that are offensive to girls and women.

Join a feminist group at school. If there isn't one, why not start one? You don't need to be an expert, but each week you could learn about some incredible women in this world doing some great things.

See if your school will think about doing something for Women's History Month or International Women's Day. Perhaps they could invite an expert in to talk about some incredible women throughout history. And don't forget that word we learnt earlier – intersectional – and include all types of women in this.

BE MORE LIKE MALALA

Malala Yousafzai was born in Pakistan and lived in a town called Mingora in the Swat Valley. In 2008, when she was eleven years old, she had to leave school because the Taliban had taken over her town, and they did not allow girls to go to school. Malala and her family knew this was wrong, and Malala spoke out against this treatment, which put her in great danger. In October 2012, a gunman got on to a bus and shot her because of her outspoken opinions. After months of surgery, Malala left hospital and went back to live with her family in the UK. Despite being at risk, she continued to campaign and fight against injustice. In 2013, along with her father, she founded the Malala Fund, which fights to ensure that every girl across the world has the opportunity and right to access education. In 2014, she was awarded the **Nobel Peace Prize** for her work and later went on to study at Oxford. **HOW CAN YOU BE MORE LIKE MALALA?**

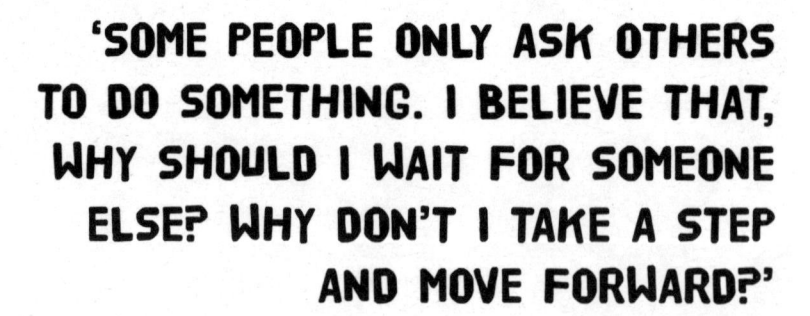

'SOME PEOPLE ONLY ASK OTHERS TO DO SOMETHING. I BELIEVE THAT, WHY SHOULD I WAIT FOR SOMEONE ELSE? WHY DON'T I TAKE A STEP AND MOVE FORWARD?'

- MALALA YOUSAFZAI

MALALA YOUSAFZAI

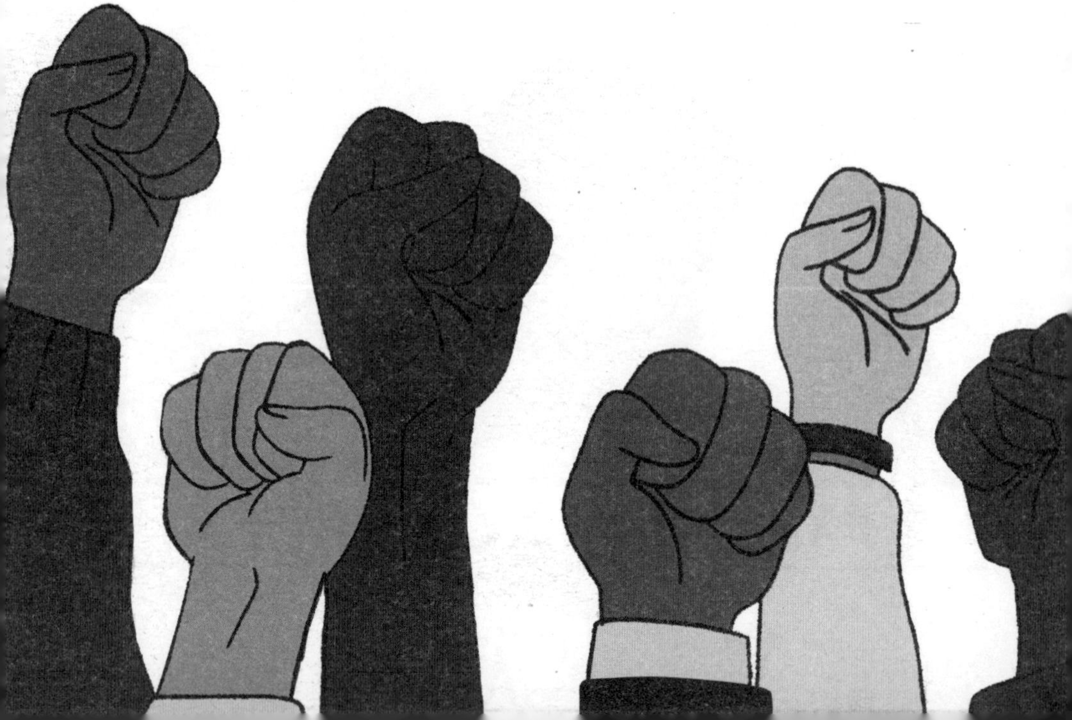

CHAPTER FOUR

everyday actions against homophobia, and celebrating all kinds of love

EQUALIT
TRANS LIVES MAT
PRIDE
EACE &
LOVE is OVE!
we are HERE we are QUEER
OUT + PROUD
DEFEND

There are so many different kinds of love. There's the love we have for our family, the love we have for our pets, the love we have for our friends and even the love we have for our favourite sporting team.

EVERYDAY MINDSET

Think about the people in your life that you love.

✦ Who are they?

ROMANTIC LOVE

When it comes to romance and partnerships, you can't predict who you will fall in love with or control who you will be attracted to. We all have different **sexual orientations** – this is means who we are attracted to or fall in love with based on gender or sex.

There are many different types of sexual orientations and some examples of these include:

HETEROSEXUAL OR STRAIGHT

This is where a man is attracted only to women or a woman is attracted only to men. You may have also heard it referred to as being **straight**.

HOMOSEXUAL OR GAY/LESBIAN

Gay is a term used to describe people who are attracted to people of the same gender – for example, a man who is attracted to other men. **Lesbian** is another word for women who are attracted to women.

BISEXUAL

Bisexual is a term used for people who are attracted to more than one gender. So, you might like both men and women at the same time or at different stages in your life.

ASEXUAL

Asexual is a term for someone who isn't attracted to anyone.

There are many more sexual orientations that we would encourage you to learn about. The truth is that sexual orientation is fluid and can change over time. It's also an individual choice and it's not for anyone else to label you. You may already know what your sexual orientation is, **or maybe you don't, and that's absolutely fine**. It is your choice whether you want to share this information with a family member/friend or not, and it's important you only do that **when you feel ready**.

LOVE CAN BE REALLY POWERFUL

The world we live in has been set up to view heterosexual/straight love as 'normal', but we know that there are lots of people who are not straight and who are a part of the LGBTQ+ community, which stands for lesbian, gay, bisexual, transgender, queer and lots of other identities, which are represented by the plus sign. Sadly, there are people who don't like people from the LGBTQ+ community, and because of this, those who are in the LGBTQ+ community have been treated badly and have not had the same rights as other people. In the UK, it is only fairly recently that gay people have been given more equal rights – for example, it wasn't until 2014 that same-sex couples could get married. In many other countries, it's still illegal to be gay and you could be sent to prison. Sounds really unfair, right?

Prejudice towards the LQBTQ+ community is called **homophobia**. It can take the form of name calling and bullying, and, in more extreme cases, violence and assault. Like most prejudice, homophobia comes from a place of not understanding or being unwilling to accept people's differences.

However, homophobia is very dangerous – it has consequences that impact the lives of LGBTQ+ people.

WHAT DOES IT MEAN TO BE TRANSGENDER?

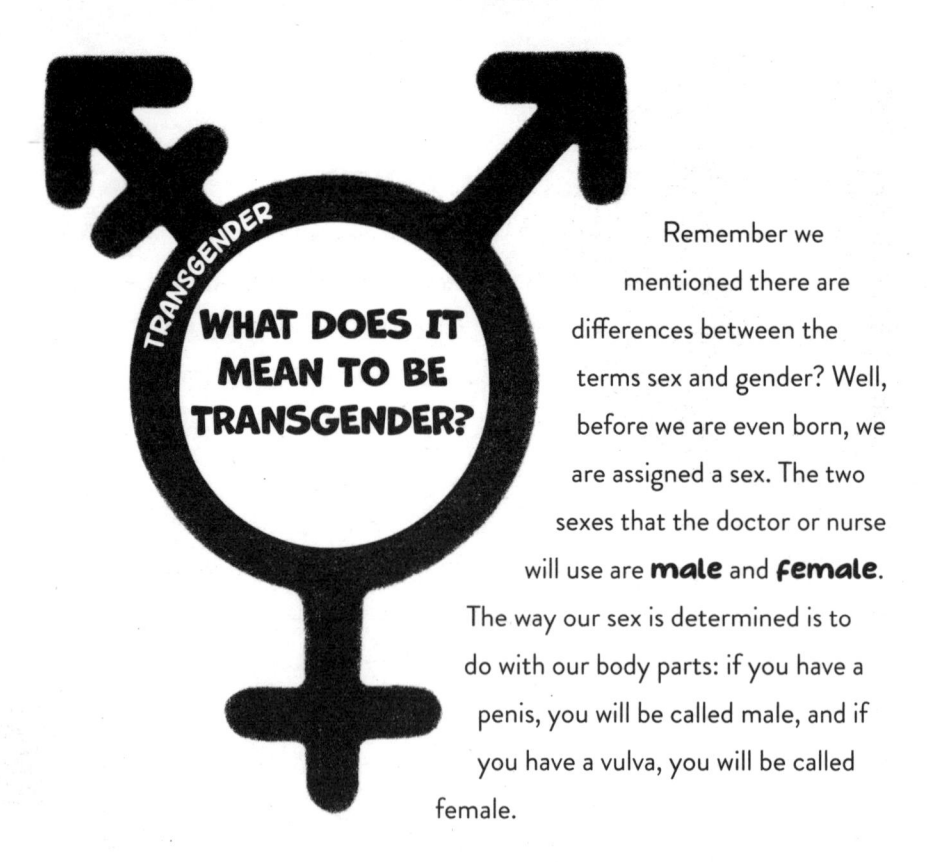

Remember we mentioned there are differences between the terms sex and gender? Well, before we are even born, we are assigned a sex. The two sexes that the doctor or nurse will use are **male** and **female**. The way our sex is determined is to do with our body parts: if you have a penis, you will be called male, and if you have a vulva, you will be called female.

Now, our gender can be the same as our sex or it can be different. Gender is the feeling you have inside, about who you are. 'Man' and 'woman' are the two most common genders, but there are others. For many people, their sex and gender will be the same – for example, someone who was assigned male at birth and feels comfortable being a man when they grow up. The word for this is **cisgender**. But for a small number of people, as they grow older, they might feel they don't match – for example, someone who was assigned male at birth but feels more like a woman than a man. This may mean they are **transgender** (**trans** for short).

NATALIE
When I was born, I was assigned female at birth, and I continue to identify as a woman, meaning I am cisgender.

FEMALE

Transphobia is where trans people are discriminated against or treated badly. There are a lot of people who don't understand this and lack empathy towards the trans community, but instead of trying to understand, they resort to bullying or even trying to stop transgender people from having the same rights as everyone else.

WHAT DOES IT MEAN TO BE NON-BINARY?

Non-binary means that a person does not identify as either a woman or a man, making them non-binary. This means they may feel like either a mix of genders or no gender at all. This also means non-binary people may use different **pronouns**. Even though non-binary people fit in the umbrella of transgender, it's important to remember that not all non-binary people are trans and not all trans people are non-binary.

NON-BINARY

WHAT ARE GENDER PRONOUNS?

We ask people's pronouns because this how we want people to

refer to us – for example, 'Natalie likes to eat ice cream and **HER** favourite flavour is pistachio.' Personal pronouns are indicators that we use to refer to ourselves. The most common pronouns are **he/him, she/her or they/them**, but there are many more that people use. It's important to ask people their pronouns before assuming someone's gender based on what they look like. It's also really good to tell people your pronouns to make others feel comfortable, for example, '**Hi, my name is Natalie, and my gender pronouns are she/her. What about you?**'

If you do get someone's pronouns wrong, it's OK – just correct yourself, apologise and move on. If someone gets your pronouns wrong, then it's OK to correct them and remind them what your pronouns are.

MEET OUR FRIEND JAMES

Remember when we said we were going to introduce some of our friends along the way? Well, we would love you to meet our friend James. James is Black and he is also a trans man.

JAMES

N+N Natalie & Naomi: *Hey, James. It's so lovely to have*

N&N: ...you join us! We are learning about the LGBTQ+ community and all about love. We're also learning more about transphobia and how it shows up. I know this is something you have experienced and you are very kindly going to share with us some of your experiences. **We know it's so important to listen to others' lived experiences, especially when it's something we might not experience ourselves.** So first, please tell us about yourself.

James: Hi! My name is James, and I use the pronouns he/him/his. I identify as a straight transgender man. One of my favourite things to do is bake, especially bread.

Natalie & Naomi: When did you first know you were trans?

James: I thought of myself as a boy as early as I can remember, which is about age four or five. At the time I didn't know the word 'trans' existed, but I knew that I was a different kind of boy to my boy mates. I began to notice that certain rules were different for me, and after a while I understood that was because of the body I was in and the expectations that come with it. One example is that I was often told I should sit with my knees together, rather than with my legs open. Another was having to wear a swimming costume rather than swimming shorts when I went swimming with my class at school.

Natalie & Naomi: How did people respond when you came out as trans? How did that make you feel?

James: I was quite scared to tell my family I was trans (this act of telling others you are LGBTQ+ is often called '**coming out**') and I was worried that I wouldn't be accepted. But afterwards I felt relieved that I wasn't hiding any more. I then felt ready to change my name to something that felt more like me, instead of the one I'd been given by my parents, who'd picked a name that was based on my **assigned sex** rather than my gender identity. Alongside this, I also asked people to refer to me using the pronouns he/him/his. At first, many people didn't understand and it took some time for them to get used to the new name I'd chosen for myself and the pronouns I was comfortable with. This was a very sad time for me because I felt quite alone, but eventually people began to **understand better** and I met other trans people who I could **talk to and share experiences with – this helped a lot.**

Natalie & Naomi: *If there are people reading this book who may be trans, what advice would you give them?*

James: First, I'd say that you're awesome! Please remember that being trans is OK.

WE'RE ALL DIFFERENT IN OUR OWN WAYS, AND BEING TRANS IS JUST ANOTHER UNIQUE DIFFERENCE.

J: When you feel ready to, **talk to someone you trust** about how you're feeling. If your parent/caregiver needs some support to understand more about being trans, it might be good to suggest looking at events run by trans organisations, where you can meet other trans children and their families. This way, you'll be able to meet other young people who may be going through similar things to you, and your family can learn more about how best to support you.

N&N Natalie & Naomi: *What advice would you give people so they can be allies to the trans community?*

J: James: It's great to ask someone what name they'd like to be called and which pronouns they prefer – this shows that you **respect their identity and want to make sure they're comfortable**. If a trans person you know isn't there and you notice people are using the wrong name or pronouns, it can be really helpful to remind others of the name and pronouns someone prefers. Of course, mistakes can happen, especially when adapting to a new name and pronouns, but it's important to **own these mistakes and correct ourselves**. Although it can be scary to stand up to others, where possible, call out bullying and speak to an adult when you witness transphobia. **It's also really important to learn from trans people's lived experiences – or the experiences of anyone within a marginalised community you aren't a part of.**

EVERYDAY ACTION

Think about the word **KINDNESS**...

- What does kindness mean to you?

- Can you think of a time when someone was kind to you?

- How did it make you feel?

Now think about how you could be kind to someone this week. It could be someone you know who is going through a hard time or it could be a family member who you love and want to show you appreciate them.
Here is an idea to help you out:

Think of something you are good at – for example, you might be really creative and enjoy making arts and crafts, or you could be like James and enjoy baking, or you might like to play sports. You can use these skills to be kind to others.

These are ours:

NATALIE

My skill: I am a really good listener and I think that's a great skill to have!

My kindness: I will use my listening skills to listen to my friends when they need someone to talk to.

NAOMI

My skill: I'm good at noticing when people don't seem happy.

My kindness: I try to cheer people up by writing a card or spending time with them.

KINDNESS IS ABOUT SHOWING EMPATHY AND STANDING UP FOR WHAT IS RIGHT!

MEET OUR FRIEND RUBY

Ruby has bright pink hair (sometimes orange) and she is here to share her experiences of being in the LGBTQ+ community.

RUBY

Natalie & Naomi: Hey, Ruby. It's so lovely to have you join us! We're learning more about homophobia and how it shows up. We know this is something you've experienced and you're very kindly going to share more with us about your experiences. So, Ruby, could you tell us about yourself?

Ruby: Hey! My name's Ruby and the pronouns I use are she/they (I'm happy with either!). I'm bisexual, which means **I'm attracted to people of all genders, and I also use the word queer to describe my sexuality, because I like how broad it is**. Some of my favourite things are wearing a ridiculous array of bright colours, eating jelly, drawing, dancing and cooking for my friends.

Natalie & Naomi: When did you first know you were gay?

Ruby: It's hard to tell when I first 'knew' I was queer (I use queer instead of gay). The first time I properly acknowledged it in myself, I was in my late teens, and it took a few more years to share that information with other people in my life and to start dating other queer people. But, in hindsight, it's something that feels like it was always there – I just didn't have the tools to fully acknowledge it. When I was growing up, there were hardly any queer role models for me to see myself in, and the world around me was so heteronormative (meaning the 'norm' was for people to be heterosexual, or straight) that I ended up hiding that part of myself for a long time. I hope nowadays this happens less with there being **more visibility and acceptance of queer people**.

Natalie & Naomi: *Have you experienced discrimination because of your sexuality? How did that make you feel?*

Ruby: I've definitely experienced discrimination, but maybe not in the ways you'd think. Gay and trans friends of mine have faced being outed at school; their parents or teachers trying to interfere with their sexuality – even being attacked on the street. I'm lucky that I've never been at risk of physical violence because of my sexuality – something many people in the queer community still face. The main discrimination I've faced has been biphobia, a particular type of discrimination against bisexual people. This includes being made to feel that I had to 'prove' my sexuality in order for it to be valid and having to fight against lots of stereotypical biphobic tropes –

like being told that I'm 'greedy' for fancying more than one gender, that I should just 'pick a side' or that I'm just saying I'm bisexual 'for attention'. While this kind of stuff isn't life-threatening in the way physical violence is, it can really take its toll on your mental health and in the past has brought up lots of shame about who I am. Sadly, this has come from other queer people as well as straight people. When discrimination comes from within the LGBTQ+ community, it can make things feel even more isolating. A big struggle that bisexual people face is invisibility – feeling like our identities are misunderstood and erased from the LGBTQ+ history and community and that we're only judged by the gender of whoever we're going out with at that time. When, actually, my sexuality isn't this thing in limbo between 'straight' and 'gay'; it's a valid identity in itself!

Natalie & Naomi: *If there are people reading this book who are gay, what advice would you give them?*

Ruby: I think it makes a huge difference having **trusted people to talk to, who won't judge you and are there for support**. That could be a trusted adult, a close friend or an LGBTQ+ youth group. Being around other people who get it is so important – it's a horrible feeling to be alone in who you are. When I found other people in the queer community, especially other people who are bi, it was a huge relief because I finally felt like I didn't have to explain myself.

Remember that you don't have to have everything about yourself figured out and that your sexuality is valid and worth celebrating! It's not something you necessarily need to share with the world – no one is entitled to know about your sexuality. But it's also not something that should be hidden in a shameful way. Like all aspects of your identity, your relationship with your sexuality will evolve over time. And if this feels scary right now, I promise that throughout your life you'll meet other LGBTQ+ people who will help you find joy, love and a sense of community.

Natalie & Naomi: *What advice would you give people to be allies to the queer community?*

Ruby: Really take the time to listen, learn and consider how someone else's experiences might cause them to relate to the world in a different way to you. It's also about being an ally within the queer community. Just because I'm queer doesn't mean I get everyone else's experiences – I hold a lot of privilege, and so it's about acknowledging that and using the privilege I have to help others.

Natalie & Naomi: *If you could recommend that someone does one thing a day to make a difference to the lives of others, what would it be?*

Ruby: Not to presume things about people in terms of their identity, but also in terms of how that identity may be for that person in particular.

THE MOMENT WE MAKE ASSUMPTIONS ABOUT OTHERS IS THE MOMENT WE STOP BEING ABLE TO BE CURIOUS AND LEARN ABOUT OTHER PEOPLE'S EXPERIENCES.

And this applies to ourselves too. I love that throughout my life I'm going to keep questioning who I am, and that that's something which will evolve. I'm a very different version of myself compared to who I was five years ago, and I'll be a different version of myself in five years' time. **I think that's really cool!**

LET'S KEEP LEARNING FROM OTHERS

It was really nice to meet some of our friends, wasn't it? **Learning from others is so important, and hearing other people's stories really helps you learn, especially when you are not in that community.** We are allies to the LGBTQ+ community, so we are always listening to others' experiences.

PRIDE

One way we support the LGBTQ+ community each year is by going to – and supporting – **Pride** events. These events take place all over the world and throughout the year. **Pride means to be proud of something**. Pride is an event to celebrate the LGBTQ+ community – it is also known as Gay Pride. By going to Pride, we are showing up and telling the LGBTQ+ community that **we support them and stand with them**. We are also currently helping to set up a Black Pride event in our hometown!

Why not ask your parent or caregiver if you can go to a Pride event? Even if you can't go to a Pride event, there are still lots of ways you can show your support – maybe you could ask your teacher if you can draw rainbow flags to stick on the walls?

HOW PRIDE BEGAN

Have you ever been to a Pride event before? If you have, you will know how bright and colourful they are and how much fun they can be – but did you know how they started?

Remember in chapter two when we spoke about different protests and we mentioned the Stonewall riots? Well, after that incident, a march took place to raise awareness of what happened at Stonewall, and this parade continued to happen year after year. It grew much bigger and has now turned into what we know as Gay Pride. Pride is a colourful event and a day to remember the events that happened in Stonewall, but also to remember the people who still are not free to this day. This has also grown into other events celebrating and highlighting people's intersectionality, such as Black Pride, Trans Pride, Black Trans Pride and more.

Did you know that we have particular months dedicated to celebrating the LGBTQ+ community? These include LGBTQ+ Pride Month, Bisexuality Visibility Month and Trans Awareness Week. Why not have a look online and see when the next Pride month is for you?

EVERYDAY ACTION

Here are some really simple things that you can do to be an ally to the LGBTQ+ community:

Practise pronouns – not everyone identifies as a boy or girl, and you can't tell how someone identifies from how they look. Instead of making assumptions about people, you could try saying something like:

HI, MY NAME IS _____ AND MY PRONOUNS ARE _____. WHAT ABOUT YOU?

HEY, CAN I ASK WHAT YOUR PRONOUNS ARE PLEASE?

Watch and read more things about LGBTQ+ people.

Take a look at the resources list at the end of the book for some suggestions.

Think about how you can be more inclusive to the LGBTQ+ community.

One example could be helping to raise awareness for the Pride events and months we have just told you about. Maybe you could start by educating your friends about it? Perhaps you can ask your school or the clubs you attend to share information about it? Or you could put a Pride flag up in your window?

Why not write some ideas down?

There are lots of incredible changemakers of the past who have paved the way for the changemakers of the future – yes, that's you!
Let's have a look at some people who have done or are doing amazing things for the LGBTQ+ community.

MEET MARSHA P. JOHNSON

As you have heard, Pride celebrations started as a protest. Marsha P. Johnson and Sylvia Rivera were crucial in **helping to look after gay and transgender people in their community as well as campaigning for their equal rights**.

MARSHA P. JOHNSON

SYLVIA RIVERA

Marsha was a very important person in the Stonewall protest that eventually led to the start of the gay rights movement. She was also a drag queen and performer, and **she inspired lots of people to be more comfortable with who they are**. Marsha and her friend Sylvia Rivera founded a charity to **help homeless transgender people** in the city, and this has influenced a lot of people to this day. Because of the Stonewall riots, people all over the world now celebrate Pride, which is a very important moment for the LGBTQ+ community, their families and their friends to come together to feel proud of who they are. **How can you be more like Marsha P. Johnson?**

'HOW MANY YEARS HAS IT TAKEN PEOPLE TO REALISE THAT WE ARE ALL BROTHERS AND SISTERS AND HUMAN BEINGS IN THE HUMAN RACE?'
- MARSHA P. JOHNSON

MEET PHYLL OPOKU-GYIMAH (LADY PHYLL)

Phyll Opoku-Gyimah, also known as Lady Phyll, is a co-founder, trustee and executive director of UK Black Pride. She is an activist who has supported and helped the LGBTQ+ community, especially those who are Black and people of colour. Her biggest achievement is setting up the first ever UK Black Pride. Pride is an event for the LGBTQ+ community to come together and celebrate being them. Black Pride is space specifically for Black LGBTQ+ members to gather and celebrate.

LADY PHYLL

Lady Phyll wants to see a world free from racism and discrimination, a world where LQTBQ+ youth can feel safe and be themselves.

How can you be more like Lady Phyll?

EVERYDAY ACTION

How about writing to those in power, for example, your local MP?

MP stands for Member of Parliament. In the UK, these are the people who are elected to represent different areas of the country in the central government, which meets in Westminster, London.

If there is an issue that you think is important, you can write to or speak to your MP. For example, maybe there is a local charity that works with young people from the LGBTQ+ community which might be shut down because it hasn't got enough money to keep running. You can write to your local MP and ask what they are going to do to help. It's not guaranteed that they will help you, but you have a right to be heard. Why not have a go? Remember to always check with your parent or caregiver before you write anything or give out your personal address.

Here's a starter template to help you:

Dear _____

My name is _____ and I live in your constituency of _____

I am writing to ask what you are doing about the issue of _____

I believe this is very important because _____

I have thought about it, and I would like to see _____

Thank you for taking the time to read this and I look forward to your response.

Yours sincerely,
_____

| ROSA PARKS | MALALA YOUSAFZAI |

| SYLVIA RIVERA | MARSHA P. JOHNSON | MARTIN LUTHER KING JR |

| JAMES | RUBY | CATHY |

'WHEN WE RISE TOGETHER WE ARE mighty'

– LADY PHYLL

RUBY BRIDGES

LADY PHYLL

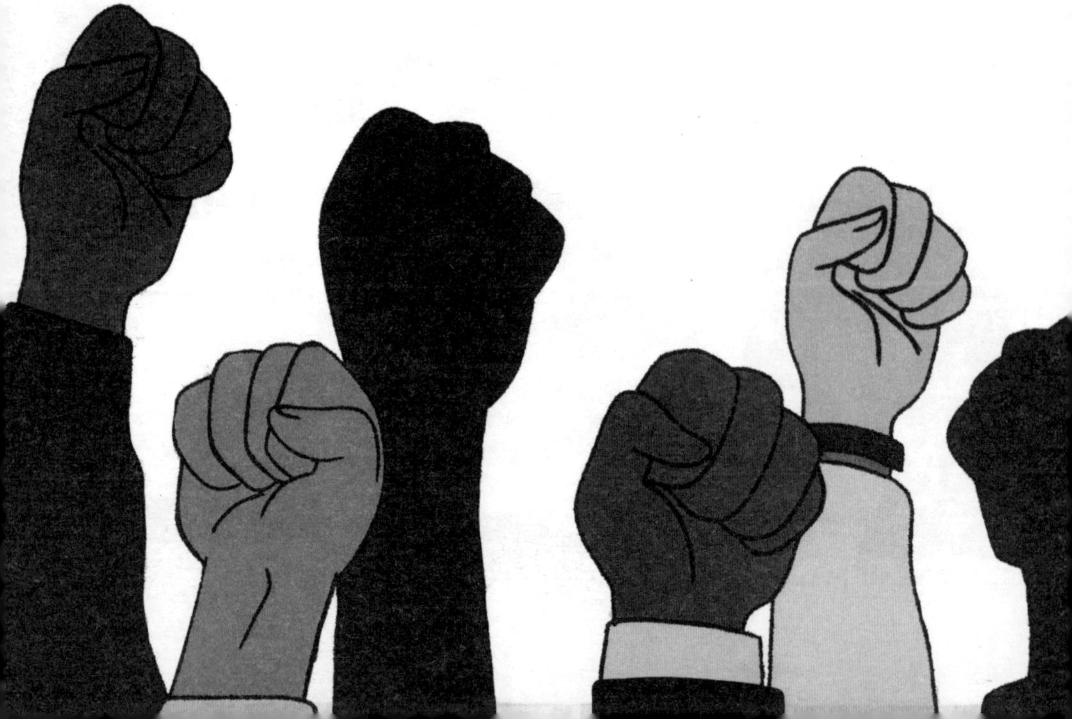

CHAPTER FIVE
Everyday action against ableism, and creating a world for all

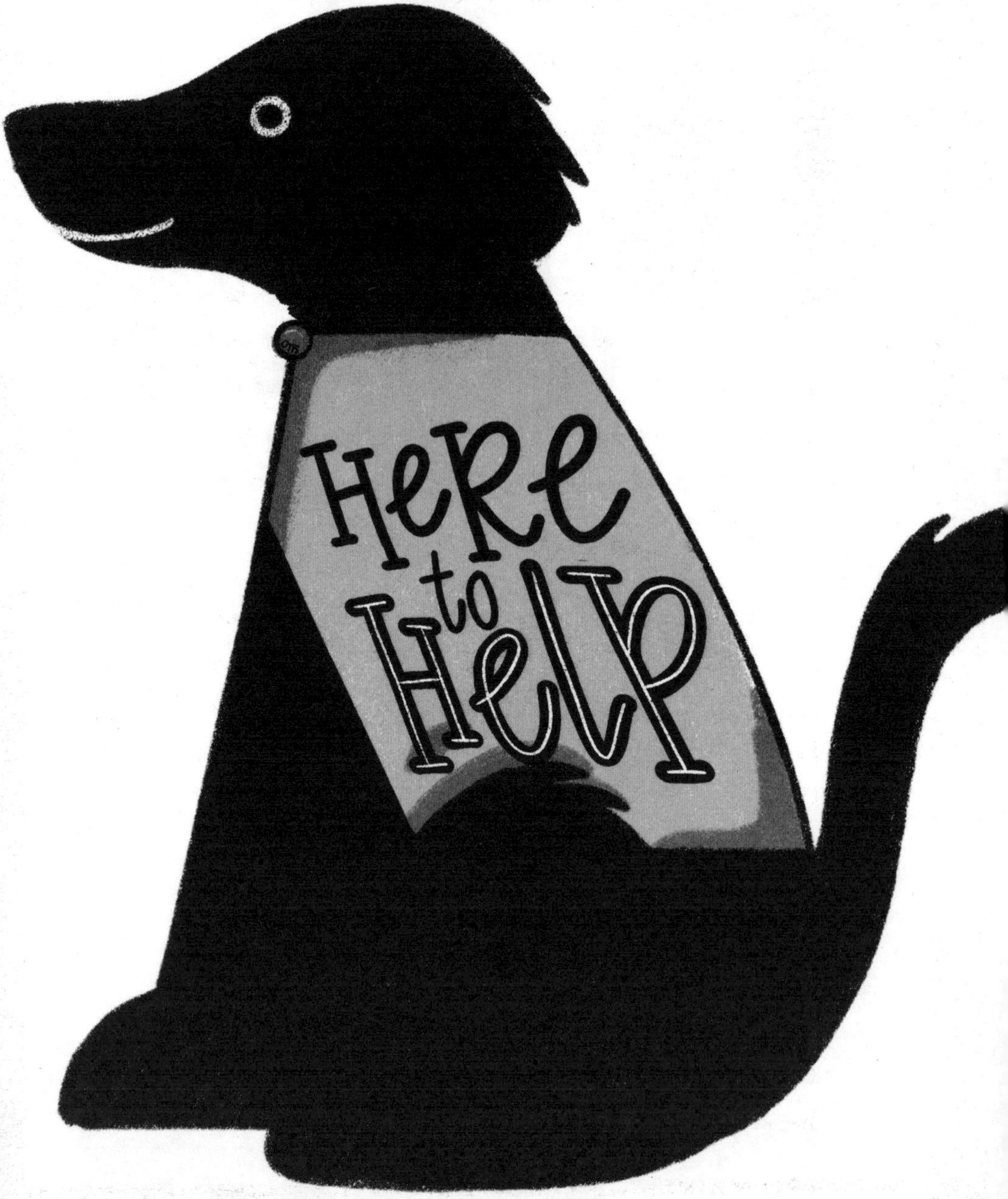
Here
to
Help

NATALIE

When I was a teenager, I found out I was dyslexic. Dyslexia is a neurological condition (which means it affects the brain) and it means that my brain processes written and spoken information differently to others, sometimes making it really hard to do things that others can do easily. For example, when writing, I find it hard to spell certain words and I find grammar really confusing. Sometimes I even put two words together to make up a whole new word, like HUGANTIC, which is a mix of huge and gigantic.

I also have problems when reading. I find it hard to remember what I have read and keep losing my place; I also might mispronounce words in my head. But one thing that I find really frustrating is that I confuse things a lot. I might have mixed up numbers or dates, so I get people's birthdays wrong! Or even people's names, which can feel really embarrassing.

WHAT IS A DISABILITY?

I soon learnt that dyslexia is a learning disability — but what is a disability, and what does it mean to be disabled? Did you know that there are over one billion disabled people in the world? There are many ways in which disabilities show up. There are physical disabilities, which are related to the movement of the body, and there are disabilities that are related to your mind. Some disabilities cannot always be seen. I am going to list some of the most common disabilities – maybe you have already heard of them? Maybe you know someone with one of these types of disability? Maybe you have a disability?

THESE ARE SOME FORMS OF DISABILITY:

VISUAL IMPAIRMENT

This is when people are blind or do not have a lot of vision. Some people may use a guide dog to help them on a daily basis, or they might use a cane, which helps people navigate their surroundings. People who are visually impaired may also use **Braille** to read or write through touch. Braille is made up of patterns of raised dots, and each pattern represents a letter of the alphabet.

DEAF OR HARD OF HEARING

This is when people can't hear at all or can only hear a little. People who are Deaf can communicate in a few different ways: by **lip reading**, by **writing notes**, through **hearing aids** (which attach a microphone, amplifier and speaker to the ear, helping to amplify sound) and through **sign language**, which is a language that uses hand gestures, body language and facial expressions.

MENTAL HEALTH CONDITIONS

Sometimes our bodies can get sick – maybe you have felt unwell at times? Maybe you have had a cold or a sickness bug? Well, sickness in the body is very common, but did you know that sometimes our brain can also become unwell? This is called having a mental illness, and it's all to do with what goes on in our brain. There are lots of mental health conditions that can affect people, including being **depressed** and having **anxiety**. Mental health conditions affect the way we feel and act.

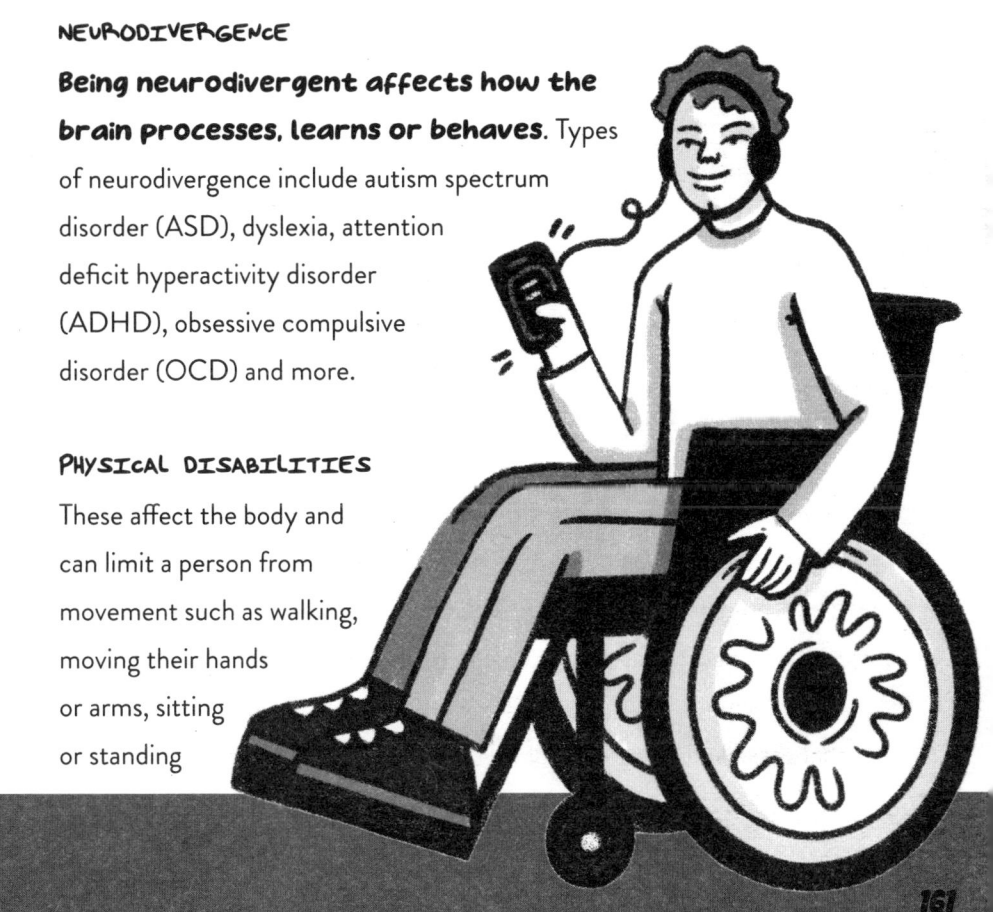

NEURODIVERGENCE

Being neurodivergent affects how the brain processes, learns or behaves. Types of neurodivergence include autism spectrum disorder (ASD), dyslexia, attention deficit hyperactivity disorder (ADHD), obsessive compulsive disorder (OCD) and more.

PHYSICAL DISABILITIES

These affect the body and can limit a person from movement such as walking, moving their hands or arms, sitting or standing and maybe being able to move their muscles. Some people may use a wheelchair or a walking stick to help them some or all of the time.

It's important to remember that some people are born with a disability and other times people can develop disabilities later in their lives.

LEARNING MORE ABOUT EACH OTHER'S DIFFERENCES IS VITAL!

EVERYDAY MINDSET

Remember when we spoke about our differences and you wrote down or thought about your identities and values? Now try writing down or thinking about three things that are special about you. They could be really quirky things, or things that no one else knows about you yet. We will go first:

NATALIE

✦ I have a birthmark that is shaped like the United Kingdom on my back!

✦ I talk to myself A LOT!

✦ I like eating raw mushrooms.

NAOMI

✦ I can make really tasty roast potatoes.

✦ I have a kind and friendly smile.

✦ I love dancing around in the kitchen to my favourite songs.

WHAT IS ABLEISM?

Ableism is discrimination against people who have a disability. Our world is set up to make life easier for people who do not have a disability. People with disabilities can face barriers when accessing basic services.

MEET ALIX

Alix uses a wheelchair to move around. There are lots of places that are difficult for them to access. Today they are heading into the city on the train. When they get to the train station, there is no lift to help them get on to the platform they need, so they have to go to another train station that does have a lift. When they get to a station that is accessible, they need to tell the train staff they are in a wheelchair to access a ramp to get on and off the train. **We need to remove the barriers that stop disabled people being a part of everyday society. To do this, we need to be more inclusive and make things more accessible.**

YOU DON'T NEED TO CHANGE TO FIT INTO THE WORLD; THE WORLD SHOULD CHANGE FOR YOU!

Accessibility refers to putting things in place so you are not excluding people because of their disability. It helps people to feel **empowered and independent**. Examples of accessibility can be having a ramp for wheelchair users, having Braille on products for blind people to read what's on the packaging and having a sign-language interpreter for the Deaf community at events or on TV.

EVERYDAY MINDSET

Imagine you are walking into a supermarket . . . When you go in, none of the items have labels on them. All the tin cans are blank, the boxes have nothing on the front and your favourite sweets or chocolate bar have no pictures of what's inside.

✦ How do you know what's in the items?

✦ Did you know that this happens to 285 million people?

✦ That's because they are visually impaired or blind. It doesn't seem very fair, does it?

EVERYDAY ACTION

Firstly, we must remember that **EVERYONE** deserves the right to respect and representation.

Think about what books you have to read at school. Are there enough books with disabled representation?

Could you talk to your teacher about that and ask for books that help us learn more about disabled people? Or bring one in from home if you already have one?

THINK ABOUT THE LANGUAGE YOU USE

Terminology is changing and evolving over time, and sadly there are still many words and phrases that are used which are ableist and offensive. You may know some already that are no longer OK to say, or you may be still saying these words without realising it yet. This all takes time and practice, but it's important to remember that **if we do cause harm by the words or names we use, we should apologise, learn from our mistakes and move on**. We should also call out others if we hear someone else say inappropriate words or names. We can do this really simply by saying, 'Excuse me, that term/name/word is actually offensive, I use ____ instead.'

COULD WE ALL COMMUNICATE IN SIGN LANGUAGE?

Have you ever learnt sign language before? Maybe you and your friends could learn it together, so you can have conversations with others, including Deaf people? Wouldn't it be cool if sign language was taught at school, like French, English or Italian? Maybe you could go a step further and create a petition to get your school to include it?

WE WOULD LOVE TO LIVE IN A WORLD WHERE EVERYONE IS ACCEPTED FOR WHO THEY ARE!

MEET OUR FRIEND CATHY

We are really excited to introduce to you our next friend, Cathy!

Cathy loves spending time with people and listening to music – especially Taylor Swift!

Natalie & Naomi: *Hey, Cathy. It's so lovely to have you join us! We are learning about the disabled community and what ableism is and how it shows up. I know this is something you have experienced and you are very kindly going to share more with us about your experiences. First up, can you tell us a little bit about yourself?*

Cathy: Hi! I'm Cathy. I'm a white disabled woman and I have two young kids who are also disabled. The three of us have **achondroplasia** (pronounced 'ay con dro play zee ah'), **which is a type of dwarfism**. I know achondroplasia is kind of hard to say and remember, so normally I just say I have dwarfism, because more people know that word! I don't really like being called a dwarf because it reminds me of *Snow White and the Seven Dwarves*, but I am happy being called a woman who has dwarfism. I'm also happy being called a disabled woman. Achondroplasia is the most common form of dwarfism, and it's the one you will have seen most in people who appear on TV, in magazines and online. Maybe you've watched Paralympian Ellie Simmonds swimming, seen actress Francesca Mills in a drama, read Sinead Burke's book *Break the Mould* or seen comedian Fats Timbo performing a funny sketch. When I was growing up, there weren't any positive representations of people with dwarfism in the entertainment industry, so **it's great that this is slowly changing now** – though there could always be more, particularly more men with dwarfism.

I love spending time with people I love, whether we're relaxing or doing fun things like going to the cinema, exhibitions or comedy shows. I love travelling and taking my kids places they've never experienced before.

N&N Natalie & Naomi: *When did you first realise you had a disability?*

C Cathy: My disability has been with me since I was in my mum's womb! I was the first person in my family to have achondroplasia (in fact, most people with my disability are born to average-height parents). I was very lucky to be born into a family that **loved and accepted me from the beginning**. My mum and dad learnt about achondroplasia, how it would affect me and the **best things they could do to support me**. They grew comfortable with my identity as a disabled person and a person with dwarfism while I was still too young to understand what was happening. Through my childhood, they talked to me about having dwarfism and introduced me to other people who have dwarfism, who I could learn from and be friends with. So, I don't really remember when I realised I was different to everyone else, because I knew before I even had the language to explain it.

Natalie & Naomi: *How did people treat you at school? How did that make you feel?*

Cathy: I had a tough time at school. I grew up in the countryside in north Norfolk in the 1990s, where most kids at my school kind of looked the same. The internet hadn't been invented yet either, so kids never saw people who didn't look or behave like them, which meant I stuck out.

Even though my parents were very quick to fight my corner and make sure I was looked after, I never really felt like I was a part of school life. I didn't have many friends and I wasn't invited to parties – or if I was, they were whole-class parties, and I'd just stand in a corner until it was home time. Other kids would only be interested in sitting next to me or being my class partner when it meant they would get special treatment, like not having to walk somewhere or getting extra time to finish an activity. I often felt very lonely, and I wondered if I would ever make any friends or find love.

Just be you

Looking back on it now, I think a lot of kids were scared of how I looked because they didn't understand dwarfism and they had learnt that they should be afraid of things they don't understand. **But we shouldn't be afraid of things we don't know. It's normal to be curious, but everyone deserves to be treated with kindness and respect, even if we don't understand why they look or behave the way they do.**

Natalie & Naomi: *What advice would you give to your younger self now you are older?*

Cathy: I would probably tell myself that **IT DOES GET BETTER**. As an adult, I am so lucky to have lots of **awesome friends**. I have also **been in love** a few times, which is something that as a child I didn't think would ever happen for me.

I would advise my younger self that **I shouldn't change who I am for other people**. I spent a lot of time when I was young pretending to like things that my classmates liked just so those people would want to be my friend. It didn't work, because while it meant I could join in conversations and maybe even make a friend or two, I was pretending to be someone I wasn't and, in the end, that didn't make me happy either.

Natalie & Naomi: *What advice would you give people to be allies to the disabled community?*

(C)

Cathy: Think about the disabled people in your life. Are there any disabled people at your school? Think about how they're treated by kids who aren't disabled – do people act scared, stare at them lots or avoid being around them? Do they have friends? It's important to learn to recognise when someone is treating a disabled person unfairly or cruelly – and if you see this happening, **it can really help to have your support**. Some disabled people might want you to be vocal in telling others that what they're doing isn't OK. Other disabled people might want you to stay silent but be privately supportive of them. **It's important to support people in the way they need, not the way you think they need.**

If you see someone disabled and you have questions, ask your parent/carer when you get home, but please don't ask us. Sometimes we might want to answer, but sometimes we are busy or, because a lot of people ask us questions, it can be tiring and not make us feel very good.

Another issue disabled people often face is inaccessibility, which happens when we can't do something or use something in the way it was intended, because it is not adapted for disabled people. For example, a wheelchair user might face inaccessibility going upstairs in a building that doesn't have a lift. And although disabled people face the most inaccessibility, everyone faces it at some point – for example, a child might face inaccessibility not being able to go on a school trip because it's too expensive.

EVERYDAY MINDSET – BY CATHY

Think about these questions to help you understand some of the barriers disabled people face on a regular basis.

- Can you think of a time when something was inaccessible to you?

- How did it make you feel?

- Were you able to make it work for you or did you have to go without?

- It might even lead you to think: what easy changes could be made to the spaces you're in to make them more accessible?

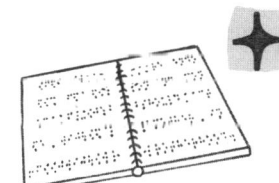

- Could a ramp be added to the entrance?

- Could Braille be added to signs?

- Could there be a place for children to go to when they feel they need quiet time?

If you can help make spaces more accessible, that's awesome. If not, it's great to spread awareness of these issues so that more people understand the barriers to society that disabled people often face.

MEET AARON ROSE PHILIP

Aaron Rose Philip is a Black transgender wheelchair-using high fashion model, who uses the pronouns she/her. At the age of only fourteen she released her book, *This Kid Can Fly: It's About Ability (Not Disability)*, detailing her experiences growing up with cerebral palsy.

She then went into modelling, where she realised there was a lack of representation of trans disabled women of colour. She is now actively working towards an **inclusive industry** and has worked for really big magazines such as *Vogue* and *ELLE*, and she has walked the runway for big modelling companies.

How can you be more like Aaron Rose Philip?

'I'D LOOK AT ALL THE SHOWS AND IT WAS SURPRISING TO SEE JUST HOW MANY PEOPLE REALLY DON'T THINK THAT DISABLED PEOPLE ALSO LIKE TO GET DRESSED UP AND FEEL GOOD. BECAUSE HOW COULD ANYONE THINK THAT? I DECIDED, "I'M GOING TO DO THIS WORK BECAUSE, WHY NOT?"'

- AARON ROSE PHILIP

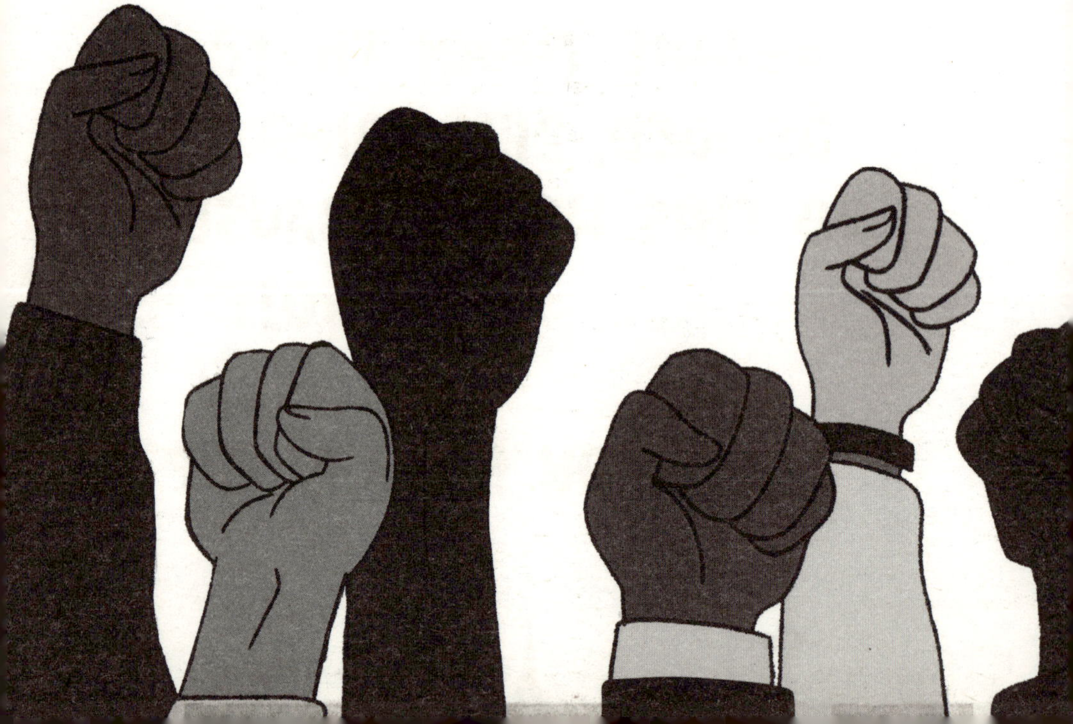

CHAPTER SIX

protecting youself from burnout, and looking out for yourself

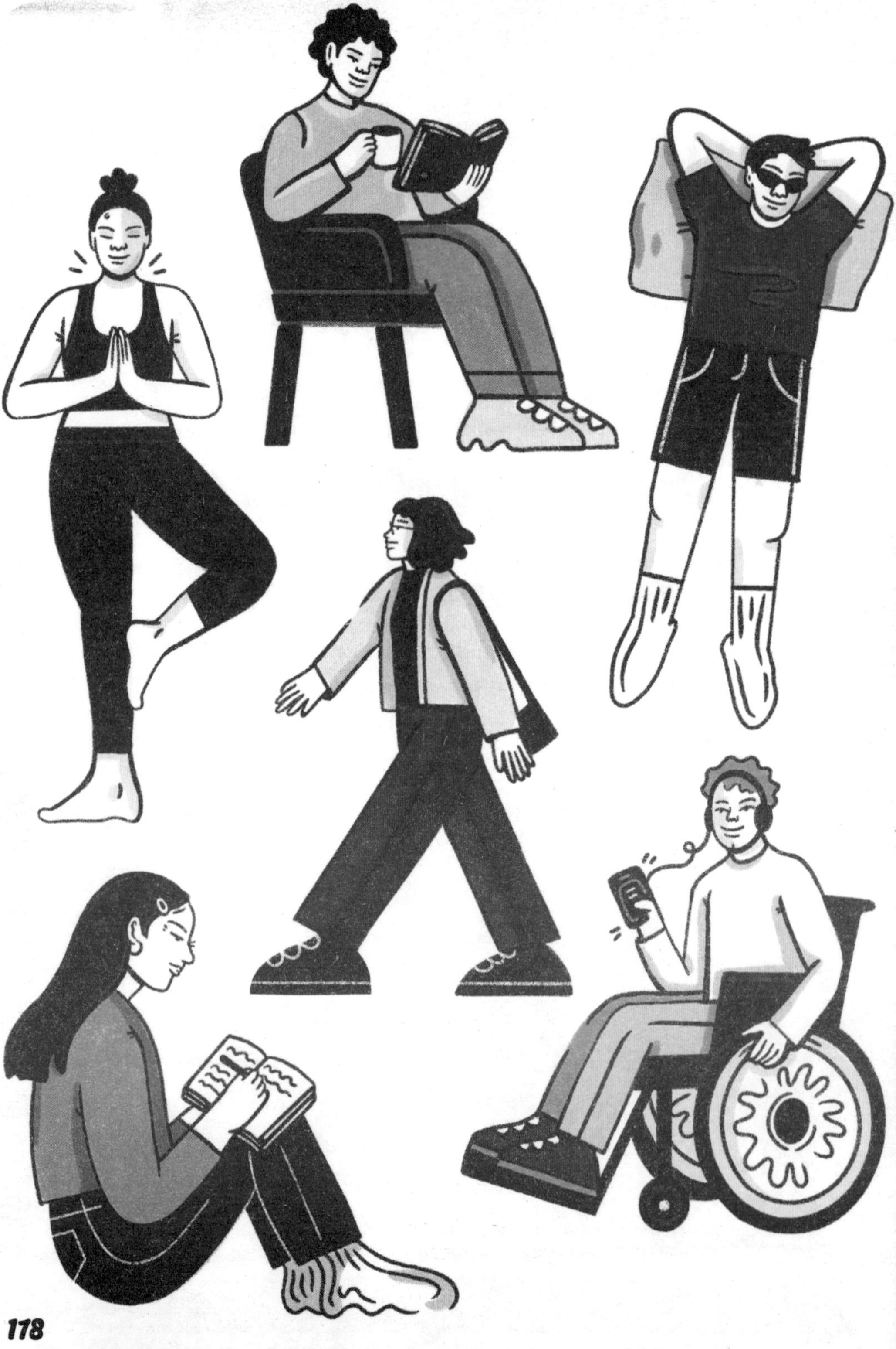

We're now nearly at the end of the book! We really hope that so far you have found it insightful and helpful, and that you've learnt some new things. But before we finish, we just want to say that this chapter is vital in your journey to being a changemaker. This is all about **looking after yourself** and **protecting yourself from burnout**. Being a changemaker can be really hard, and it can affect us mentally and physically. To avoid this, we need to put some things in place **to protect ourselves**.

I DON'T KNOW WHERE TO START

It can sometimes feel that there are a lot of issues to think about and overcome in our world and there's not much that we can do about it. Has your bedroom ever got so messy that you give up trying to keep it tidy? Once toys are out and books and clothes are flung everywhere, it becomes harder and harder to start sorting things out.

NAOMI

When my bedroom is really messy, I try to focus on one bit at a time — so, for example, I'll just look for all the socks to put away. It suddenly feels much more manageable than trying to do everything at once. That's not to say you ignore the books and pants and whatever else is lying about, but sometimes you have to put your attention on one thing at a time, otherwise it's overwhelming.

WE NEED TO TAKE THINGS ONE STEP AT A TIME

There are many issues in this world, and they can affect both individuals and groups of people. For us, one of the ways we can make a change is by helping people to understand more about racism and then how to fight against it.

After we set up our Instagram account @everydayracism_, it snowballed and grew dramatically. It grew so fast we didn't know how to keep up, and we were constantly playing catch-up. We soon learnt there were people in this world who didn't like what we were doing and would say really nasty things to us because of it. The online world is a complicated place, and even though we can do some really good things online, the internet also allows people to say and do horrible things because they are hiding behind a keyboard – some people call them keyboard warriors or trolls. We were getting a lot of hate from people and that affected our mental health and made us really sad. It would also make us anxious about sharing things online. So we had to make sure we were looking after ourselves.

THERE IS NO BETTER GIFT YOU CAN GIVE YOURSELF THAN SELF-CARE

Self-care is vital for when you're being an ally and standing up for others. Knowing what self-care looks like for you means that you are one step ahead when you need to look after yourself. Self-care is something you do in order to recharge your batteries! You know when you use a tablet or a Nintendo Switch and after a while the battery dies, and you have to plug it in and recharge it? Well, that's kind of how we as humans work! It's hard to recharge sometimes, especially when things are busy. We might feel we need to keep going, but it's so important to listen to our bodies and rest on a regular basis.

There are many ways we can plug ourselves in to recharge. One of the obvious ways is our sleep routine – because it is crucial that our bodies have time to rest and restore for the following day. Our bodies need to recharge, just like our mobile phones!

EVERYDAY ACTION

Do you have a sleep routine? Here are some tips for getting a good night's sleep:

- Try not to go to bed too late, and make sure you aim for about eight hours of sleep each night

- If possible, avoid technology or TV just before you go to bed.

- Read a book (you may be reading this book right now as you prepare to sleep – excellent choice!)

- Spend some time journalling and writing about your day or listening to music

- Share your routine with the people you live with so they can help you stick to it

NATALIE

Another part of self-care is thinking about the things that help you relax. It's so good to have an idea of what this looks like, because we all have days when we just don't feel ourselves and it can be really unexpected. Sometimes I wake up in the morning and just feel really overwhelmed with everything I do – it can really get on top of me, so knowing what my self-care looks like can help me get out of that headspace.

YOUR SELF-CARE MATTERS BECAUSE YOU MATTER

EVERYDAY ACTION

Think of some self-care ideas. Why not write these on a sticky note and put them somewhere where you can be reminded of them? You will be surprised how easily you might forget them otherwise.

Here are some questions to help you:

- What makes you smile?
- What relaxes you?
- Where do you feel most calm?
- Who do you feel most safe with?
- What kind of music makes you feel relaxed?
- What activity do you enjoy doing the most?

Here are some of our friends' tips on self-care and what they like to do to look after themselves:

James: I love to go for long walks and listen to audiobooks to relax. I also play the guitar, read fiction books and bake.

Cathy: My self-care tips are making sure you go outside and move your body every day, even if it's just in the garden, and having a few people you can talk to when you need to. If I stay home and don't do any exercise at all, I'm much more likely to feel sad or annoyed by the end of the day. I have friends I chat to for different problems, and it really helps to take the weight off.

Ruby: Swimming! I live by the sea, and whenever I feel stressed or sad, I jump in the sea and everything feels a bit better. There's something about floating in water that makes me feel calm and centred; it's a moment when I can spend time alone in nature, and I feel like it charges me up to tackle the rest of my day. I also really love singing. I joined a choir a few years ago and singing with other people lifts my mood like nothing else. It's a time to come together and create a beautiful sound as a team, and it helps to remind me of the power of being part of a community.

ALWAYS BE KIND TO YOURSELF

WE ARE ALL HUMANS, AND HUMANS GET THINGS WRONG SOMETIMES!

One thing we want to remind you of when being a changemaker is that we all make mistakes! **Every single one of us**. Making mistakes can make us feel sad and frustrated, but you know what? **Making mistakes is important because it gives us opportunities to learn and grow**.

GROW FROM MISTAKES, AND DON'T MAKE THE SAME MISTAKE TWICE!

No one is perfect. **PERFECTION DOES NOT EXIST** – even though it would be nice, right? So let's remember we are all human and remind ourselves of that word we spoke about at the beginning of the book – **empathy**. We can have empathy towards ourselves.

EVERYDAY MINDSET

Write down some things that you love about being you and that you want to celebrate.

Here are ours:

NATALIE

I love that I am outgoing and I have a nice smile.

I love that I work hard every day to make the world a better place.

I love that I love my family and my cat and that I am kind to others.

NAOMI

I love that I have two children who I love and who love me back.

I love that I get to do a job that I really enjoy.

I love that I have been able to write books that can help other people.

If you write yours down too, then you can come back to your list at times when you are feeling discouraged or sad.

FIND YOUR SUPPORT NETWORK

We need people around us to help us look after ourselves, because we can't always do it alone. Think about who the people in your support network are. These are the people who listen to you, who you trust, who laugh with you and who will challenge you. For us, our support network is our family, our mum and our friends. You may not have the same network as us – sometimes close family isn't where we always feel the most comfortable – so why not think of other people, such as a teacher, a club leader or your friends.

EVERYDAY ACTION

Draw your support network on a piece of paper.

- Draw a spider diagram with 'you' in the middle and your support network in surrounding circles.

- Write down different names of people who are important to you who can be in your support network.

Talk to those people in your support network and tell them about being a changemaker and what that might look like for you. **How do you need them to support you?**

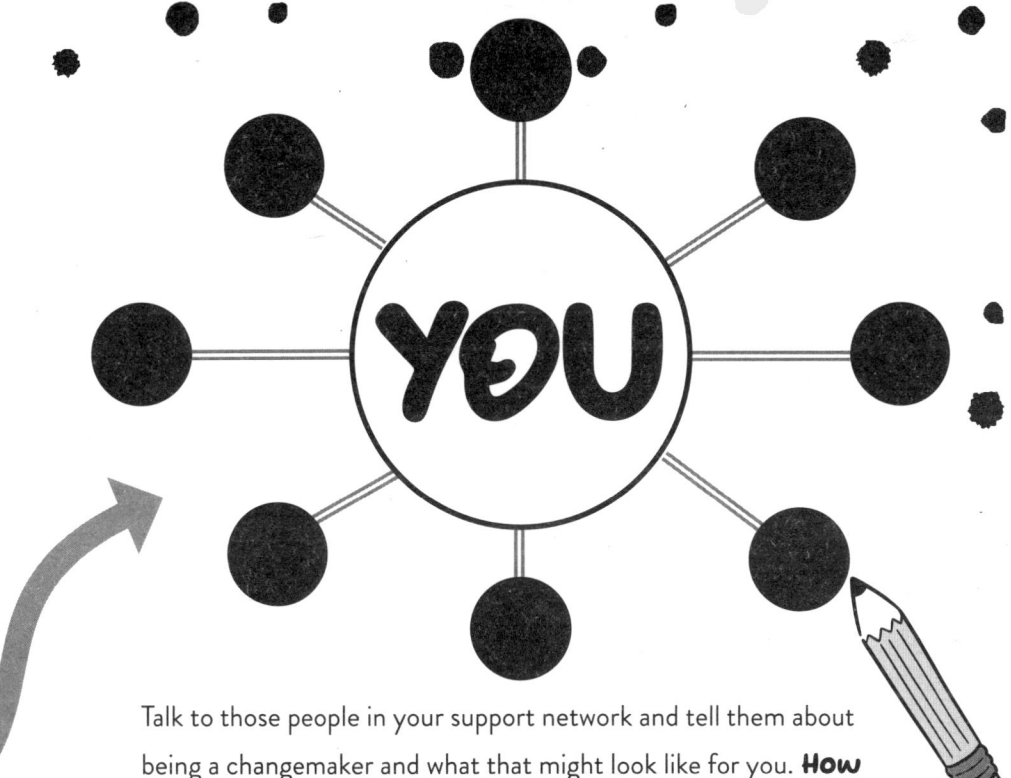

IT'S IMPORTANT TO HAVE PEOPLE WHO SUPPORT YOU

People who make a difference aren't always known by everyone. They can often go unnoticed or unappreciated, so it can really help to make sure you have some self-care, self-love and people you love and trust around you, because being a changemaker is lifelong work! Daily check-ins with yourself are so important. Even if it's as simple as asking yourself, 'How am I feeling today?' or 'What do I need today?'

The most important thing is to keep listening and keep learning – you have got this!

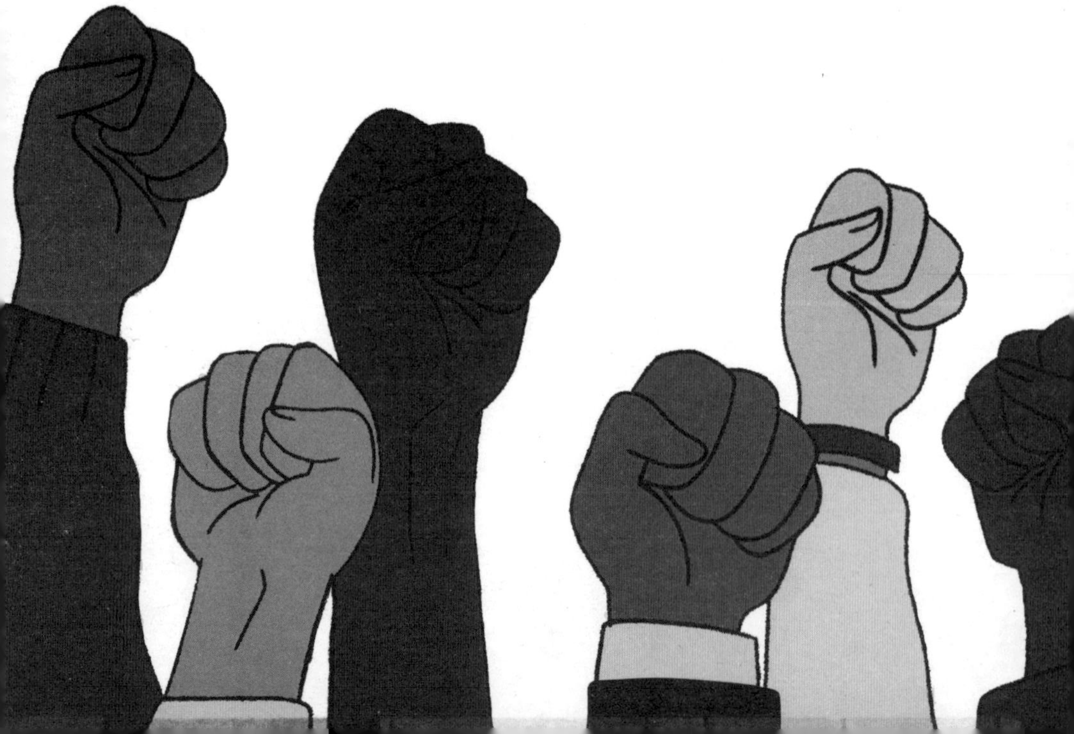

BE A CHANGEMAKER

ROSA PARKS

MARTIN LUTHER KING JR

MALALA YOUSAFZAI

RUBY BRIDGES

MARSHA P. JOHNSON

SYLVIA RIVERA

Well, you made it. We really hope you have **learnt some new things** while reading this book and have **taken some practical tips** away on how to be a changemaker.

There are things in life that can seem really overwhelming, but the most important thing to remember is that **we have the power to change things one little step at a time**. Throughout this book, we have learnt about some types of discrimination and how it shows up, and we have weaved in some everyday action and everyday mindset tips that will help us to be allies to marginalised communities.

WE HAVE THE POWER TO CHANGE THINGS!

There may be some injustices that you feel really passionate about, and you might choose to take up the cause to fight against these injustices, which is great. You may decide there are other areas of injustices we haven't spoken about in this book that you want to research, for example, climate change and how we can help save our planet. **Whatever it is, we are just so pleased you want to start somewhere, and we would encourage you to write down where you want to start.**

So we will end the book with one last everyday action . . .

You may feel you have more than one area you want to fight for, and that's totally OK too.

EVERYDAY ACTION

Think about how you might begin your changemaking journey. Here are some questions to help you:

- ✦ What is the injustice that you want to look into?

- ✦ Why do you feel passionate about this?

- ✦ What are some ways you can get involved in taking action?

- ✦ What is your self-care tip for yourself?

NATALIE
There was a time in my life when I could have kept quiet and not said anything when I saw a racist incident happen, but I didn't. I was loud, bold and messy — but you know what? It paid off, and I am so proud of myself for using my voice to speak out and become a changemaker.

WE ARE SO PROUD OF YOU!

We are proud of you for **reading this book**, for **thinking about and writing down the everyday action plans** and for **doing the everyday mindsets**, and we are so proud of you **for being YOU**!

And remember: be compassionate and kind to others, be kind to yourself, think about your own safety before taking action, be OK with getting things wrong and keep learning from others, especially those who have different lived experiences to you. Together, we can all be . . .

CHANGEMAKERS.

GLOSSARY

ableism: Discrimination against disabled people.

accessibility: Putting things in place so you are not excluding people, particularly because of disability.

ally: Someone who stands up for and supports someone's difference – even when they don't have to.

anti-racism: Actively helping to fight racism (not just saying that you're not racist) – this can include educating yourself through reading, protesting, campaigning and challenging racism when you see or hear it happen.

asexual: Someone who isn't sexually attracted to anyone else (but may still want to be in a romantic relationship with someone).

assigned sex: Before we are born, we are assigned a sex. The two sexes that the doctor or nurse will use are 'male' and 'female'. Sex is determined by our body parts; if you have a penis, you will be called male, and if you have a vulva you will be called female.

bias: When we form a judgement or an opinion on someone or something before we have even got to know them.

bisexual: Someone who is attracted to more than one gender – they might be attracted to both men and women at the same time or at different stages in their life.

cisgender: A person whose gender identity is the same as the sex they were assigned at birth.

classism: When people are treated differently based on their social status.

colonialism: Colonialism is when one country or nation takes over and controls other lands or countries. It's usually a richer country that takes control of a less powerful country.

disability: Any condition of the body or mind that makes it more difficult for the person with the condition to do certain activities and interact with the world around them.

ethnicity: Belonging to a group of people who are connected because of things they have in common, such as language, culture, religion and so on.

feminism: Wanting all genders to have equal rights and opportunities – for example, for women to have the same pay as men, to be taken seriously for certain jobs that people think only men should do, to have the right to make decisions about their own bodies and to be able to make the choices they want to make rather than men making the choice for them.

gay: A term used to describe people who are attracted to people of the same gender – for example, a man who is attracted to other men.

gender: Gender is the feeling we have inside, about who we are, and is often expressed through the clothes we wear, how we wear our hair and the way we speak. Examples of gender are male, female and non-binary.

heterosexual: When a man is attracted to a woman, or a woman is attracted to a man – you may have also heard it referred to as being straight.

homophobia: Discrimination against people who are gay.

internalised racism: When Black people and people of colour don't like themselves or something about themselves because of their race, ethnicity and culture. This is because of the negative messages that they might see or hear about themselves.

intersectionality: A term used by Professor Kimberlé Crenshaw to help us understand the ways we all have our own unique ways of experiencing discrimination and privilege.

Islamophobia: Prejudice against Islam or people who are Muslim.

lesbian: A term used to describe women who are attracted to women.

LGBTQ+: Stands for lesbian, gay, bisexual, transgender, queer and lots of other identities, which are represented by the plus sign.

mixed race: Having parents from two or more ethnic backgrounds. The term 'mixed race' is commonly used in the UK. Other ways that mixed-race people may identify might include biracial, multiracial, multi-ethnic and mixed.

nationality: This refers to your country of citizenship – it is sometimes the place you live, and it will usually be the place you have on your passport.

non-binary: Someone who does not identify as the sex they were assigned at birth, but also doesn't identify as either male or female, making them non-binary. This means they may feel like a mix of genders or no gender at all and express themselves how they feel most comfortable.

people of colour: People who are not white – often shortened to POC.

prejudice: Having an unfriendly opinion or feeling towards someone without knowing anything about them.

privilege: When a person has an advantage over others because of their identity.

pronouns: Indicators of how we refer to ourselves. Examples can be she/her or he/him or they/them.

race: The physical characteristics that define you and make you part of a group, for example, skin colour, hair colour and hair texture. The word 'race' is thrown around a lot, but it doesn't actually exist. It was something invented around the seventeenth century to divide people. By putting people in different categories, it allowed certain groups to have power over others. The simple fact is that there is only one race – the human race.

racism: When someone is discriminated against because of the colour of their skin, their culture or their language.

sexism: When a person is treated unfairly because of their gender or sex.

Sinophobia: Racism towards Chinese people and their culture.

stereotype: When we have an idea or belief about groups of people.

systemic racism: When groups or organisations treat people with different colour skin unfairly. This isn't as much about one person being mean to someone else, but it's about how groups or organisations, for example, the police, schools or workplaces, treat groups of people. It can happen when racist ideas are built into policies, laws, attitudes and behaviour.

transgender: When someone's gender identity does not match the sex they were assigned at birth.

transphobia: When trans people are discriminated against or treated badly.

white privilege: A type of privilege that means your skin colour won't be something that affects you negatively in life (but it doesn't mean your life is easy because you are white).

white supremacy: A belief that white people are better and, because of this, white people are given the ability to make decisions about things like money and laws. One of the ways to end racism is by giving different people the opportunity to make decisions.

RESOURCES

ONLINE

Pop'n'Olly www.popnolly.com
Olly and his team help teach people about equality and diversity and how to combat prejudice within the LGBTQ+ community.

Queer Kid Stuff www.queerkidstuff.com
Queer Kid Stuff make videos, newsletters and resources to help people learn more about LGBTQ+ and social justice issues.

CBBC Proud to Be Me www.bbc.co.uk/cbbc/joinin/bp-what-makes-you-proud
Here you will find some inspiring young people sharing why they are proud to be themselves.

ORGANISATIONS

Stonewall Young Futures https://www.stonewall.org.uk/young-futures
A dedicated youth team within Stonewall who campaign for LGBTQ+ rights and provide information and resources, including on mental health.

Childline www.childline.org.uk
Offers a free, confidential service for young people to talk to counsellors via phone, online chat or email.

Kids of Colour www.kidsofcolour.com
Kids of Colour create spaces to challenge the racism that young people experience.

ACKNOWLEDGEMENTS

We want to say thank you to our wonderful agent, Silè Edwards, and the fantastic team at Hachette who have been so incredible to work with, with a special thanks to Laura Horsley, Victoria Walsh, Emily Thomas and Beth McWilliams. Plus the very talented illustrators, Kelly Malka and Jasmin Sehra, and designer, Pippi Grantham-Wright.

Finally, thank you to Amadi and Vicki from MWW for all your support.

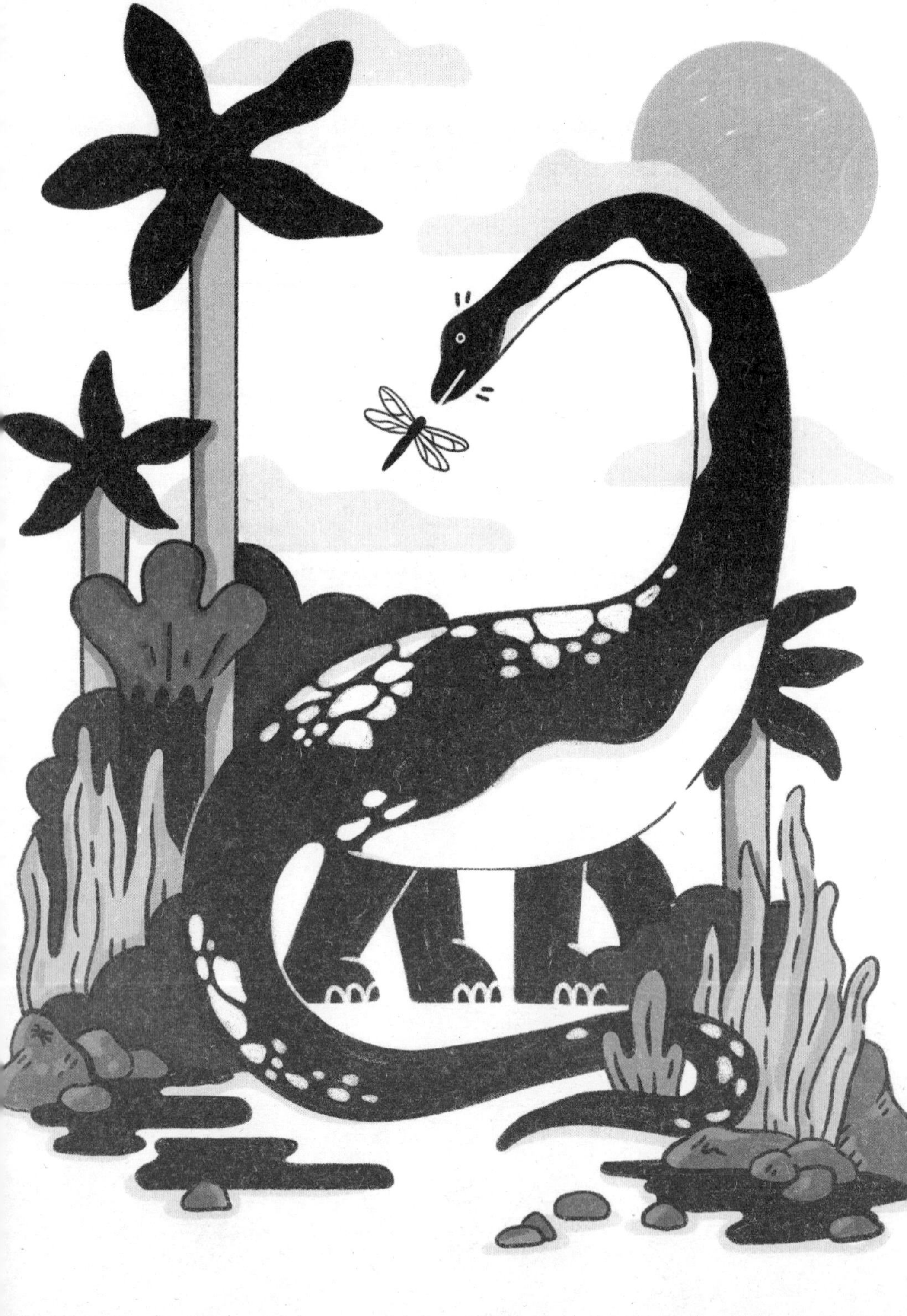